GLOBAL UNDERSTANDINGS

A Framework for Teaching and Learning

CHARLOTTE ANDERSON WITH SUSAN K. NICKLAS AND AGNES R. CRAWFORD

ASSOCIATION FOR SUPERVISION AND CURRICULUM DEVELOPMENT
ALEXANDRIA, VIRGINIA

Association for Supervision and Curriculum Development
1250 N. Pitt Street • Alexandria, Virginia 22314
Telephone: (703) 549–9110   FAX: (703) 549–3891 or 836–7921

The Authors

Charlotte C. Anderson is President, Education for Global Involvement, Inc., North Lakeside Cultural Center, 6219 N. Sheridan Rd., Chicago, IL 60660. (312) 465–6122. Susan K. Nicklas is ASCD's Director of Field Services and Agnes R. Crawford is ASCD's Assistant Director of Professional Development.

ASCD publications present a variety of viewpoints. The views expressed or implied in this publication should not be interpreted as official positions of the Association.

The development of this curriculum framework was supported by a grant from the Longview Foundation for Education in World Affairs and International Understanding, Reston, Virginia.

Printed in the United States of America.
Cover design by Karen Monaco

Nancy Modrak, *Managing Editor, ASCD Books and Editorial Services*
Julie Houtz, *Senior Associate Editor*
Biz McMahon, *Assistant Editor*
Gary Bloom, *Manager, Design and Production Services*
Stephanie Justen, *Production Coordinator*
Karen Monaco, *Senior Graphic Designer*
Valerie Sprague, *Desktop Publishing Specialist*

ASCD Stock No.: 1–94215
Price: $14.95
ISBN: 0-87120-240-9

Library of Congress Cataloging-in-Publication Data
Anderson, Charlotte C.
    Global understandings : a framework for teaching and learning /
    Charlotte C. Anderson with Susan K. Nicklas and Agnes R. Crawford.
        p.   cm.
    Includes bibliographical references (p.   ).
    ISBN 0-87120-240-9
    1. International education—United States. I. Nicklas, Susan K.   II. Crawford, Agnes R.
III. Association for Supervision and Curriculum Development.   IV. Title.
LC1090.A65   1994
370.19'6'0973—dc20   94-38856
                                                            CIP

GLOBAL UNDERSTANDINGS
A Framework for Teaching and Learning

Acknowledgments

This framework is the culmination of the work of many individuals over several years. ASCD Affiliate Global Commissioners contributed their time, expertise, and enthusiasm to make this project a reality. The ASCD Global Education Network and its members have provided constant support and encouragement.

The schools listed below worked with ASCD to pilot the framework. Their staffs, administration, and local communities helped to ensure that the framework is a practical, useful guide for classroom teachers. We greatly appreciate their work.

Amherst Elementary Schools
  Amherst, New Hampshire
Broward Elementary School
  Tampa, Florida
Byck Elementary School
  Louisville, Kentucky
Federal Way Public Schools
  Federal Way, Washington
Hans Christian Andersen Contemporary
  Elementary School
  Minneapolis, Minnesota
Helen Herr Elementary School
  Las Vegas, Nevada
International School of Amsterdam
  Amsterdam, The Netherlands
Joshua Eaton Elementary School
  Reading, Massachusetts
Lincoln Elementary School
  Gering, Nebraska
Lincoln International Studies School
  Kalamazoo, Michigan
Nativity Catholic Academy
  Washington, D.C.

Union Elementary and David R. Gaul Middle Schools
  Union, Maine
University Elementary School
  Bloomington, Indiana
Westminster Elementary School
  Atlanta, Georgia
Wiley International Magnet Elementary School
  Raleigh, North Carolina

The section of this book entitled "Performance Assessment in Global Education" was developed by the Stanford Program on International and Cross Cultural Education (SPICE) at Stanford University. Jane Boston, Director of SPICE, and Kyo Yamashiro, Research Assistant, SPICE, were its principal authors. Particular thanks go to Robin Miyahara, Administrative Assistant, SPICE, for her support and help with this project. Special appreciation is extended to the following individuals who generously shared their experience with performance assessment and provided many of the specific examples included in the section: Jeffrey L. Brown, Executive Director, Global Learning, Inc., Union, New Jersey; "Peg" (Margaret) Hill, Coordinator of History-Social Science, San Bernardino County Superintendent of Schools; Constance Miller Manter, Maine Department of Education, Maine Geographic Alliance; Phyllis Perkins, Global Education Representative, Monroe County Community School Corporation, University School, Bloomington, Indiana; Siegfried Ramler, Director of the Wo International Center, Punahou School, Honolulu, Hawaii; Douglas G. Schermer, Briggs Elementary School, Maquoketa, Iowa; Barbara Stanford, Arkansas International Center, University of Arkansas at Little Rock.

Part One

THE FRAMEWORK

1

The Rationale for a Global Framework

■ The Changing World

Young people around the world are growing up in polyethnic and multicultural nations. These nations find themselves functioning in an increasingly integrated global system. On the cusp of the 21st century, all citizens of Planet Earth find ourselves extensively involved in a global system that touches every aspect of our lives. The food we eat, the clothes we wear, and the people we meet reflect the interrelatedness of each facet of our lives.

Most of us were educated into and have experienced throughout our lifetimes a world quite different from the one that our children will know. Living in a world characterized by the increasing pluralism of localities operating within the context of global interdependence is a significantly different life experience from that of most adults on this planet. Our children will need new skills and attitudes to function productively in this different environment. They will need an understanding of and appreciation for the global nature of life in the future.

The global challenges confronting future generations will surely continue to revolve around the global issues we have just begun to confront: human rights, environmental relationships, conflict, and social and physical well-being. During our children's lives, however, these issues will undoubtedly become more intense and more personal as a natural result of the dual conditions of diversity and interdependence. Incidences of ethnic conflict, for example, will move—with the aid of communication and transportation technologies—almost instantaneously across the globe, igniting emotions in disparate locations wherever people of the same or sympathetic ethnicities are located. An environmental crisis in a given location will be broadcast immediately around the world and recognized as both a global and a local issue. People will confront one another with accusations of responsibility and proposals for solutions that will often be diametrically opposed.

■ An Integrated Approach

This new global reality intensifies the difficulties that we face in educating our young. It clearly calls for a global education that permeates the curriculum and provides a far more extensive and sounder education than schools have previously provided about the nature of the human species, the planet that we call home, and the ways we organize ourselves on the face of the Earth. Such an education is necessarily a comprehensive, cross-curricular, and interdisciplinary enterprise requiring integration of the humanities, the sciences, and the social sciences.

The humanities, for example, offer insights into the rich cultural variations in the arts and literature that the species has generated. The sciences provide children with information on the fundamental components of life and the intricacies of the planet's life support systems. A comprehensive global education draws on the humanities, the sciences, and the social sciences to reveal that human societies— across space and over time—have differed significantly in their relationships with the environment and with each other.

If our young people are to meet the global challenges confronting humankind in the 21st century, they must have a global education that begins in the primary grades and is addressed throughout the curriculum. Only by receiving a sound foundation of fundamental knowledge about life on this planet will children have at hand the information they need to identify and address critical global challenges. Only by developing underlying skills and caring capacities will children possess the confidence and commitment to use such information for improving the human condition.[1] Only through practice in carefully designed, developmentally appropriate tasks related to critical global challenges will children acquire the competencies that are the building blocks for civic action in meeting global challenges throughout their lives.[2]

This framework is a guide for developing experiences for young people that will prepare them for the world of today and tomorrow. It cuts across the curriculum by focusing on our fundamental knowledge about human beings, Planet Earth, the specific nations in which children live, and the interrelated world. It promotes the development of key competencies to meet global challenges. Not only does the framework *allow* for cross-curricular and interdisciplinary attention, it *demands* it. All curriculum areas and educational institutions must be involved if our progeny are going to be able to meet the challenges that we, their ancestors, bequeath to them.

[1] The caring capacities and the information–acquiring, communicating, and processing skills were systematically articulated in *Skill Development in Elementary Social Studies: A New Perspective* by Barbara J. Winston and Charlotte C. Anderson, jointly published by ERIC Clearinghouse for Social Studies and the Social Science Education Consortium in 1977. The competencies associated with caring capacities have been used for resource and program evaluation by global education projects.

[2] Much of this analysis of global education competencies draws on work done earlier by the author with colleagues Lee Anderson and Barbara Winston in the development of *Windows On Our World*, a K–6 social studies program with a cross-curricular global perspective published by Houghton Mifflin in 1976.

■ Using This Framework

The ASCD Framework for Global Education is just that—a framework. It is neither a curriculum for global education nor a compendium of global education activities. It is a guide to assist schools and teachers in developing educational plans for students. It provides a global lens through which lessons, curriculum, and experiences can be conceived. It identifies essential global concepts that should permeate every plan designed for students. It prompts educators to use a global perspective as they develop the setting, culture, and experiences for students in the school environment.

The framework begins with an exposition of four messages for students. These messages are the foundation for thinking globally; they are the heart and substance of the global curriculum. Each message is described in detail with suggested outcomes that will result from their infusion into all aspects of the curriculum. Explicit in the messages and outcomes is the notion that lifelong learning skills are an integral part of a global education.

We include several model units to illustrate the power of an integrated approach to curriculum and instruction and its particular value in global education. These units exemplify a global perspective within existing requirements for content and skills.

We also provide information on the development of authentic assessments. Educators living in a globally interrelated world need assessment practices appropriate for their unique school and class setting that can provide information on the achievement of global goals.

We conclude with a bibliography of resources that support the framework. These resources will help globally oriented educators plan instruction and connect with others who believe our children will harvest the fruits of the future if we work together now.

2

An Overview of the Framework

The realities of a globally interrelated and culturally diverse world of the 21st century require an education for all students that will enable them to see themselves as

---

HUMAN BEINGS

whose home is

PLANET EARTH

who are citizens of

A MULTICULTURAL SOCIETY

living in an increasingly

INTERRELATED WORLD

and who

LEARN, CARE, THINK, CHOOSE, and ACT

to celebrate life on this planet
and
to meet the global challenges confronting humankind

The messages inherent in this perspective form the basis of the ASCD Global Education Framework. When we emphasize these messages in the lessons we design, we help students to recognize the commonalities in all human beings, to become effective caretakers of our planet, to honor human diversity, and to work together for the benefit of all. The

understanding that we must learn these messages, care about them, think about them, choose them as our own, and act upon them will result in a global education worthy of our future, one that will maximize human rights, the quality of the environment, and the health and well-being of all.

■ Powerful Messages to Students

Message 1: "You are a HUMAN BEING."

Young people who grow up seeing themselves as human beings related to all other human beings have the potential for developing responsive, humane institutions and technologies to enhance the human condition throughout the world. As they explore the nature of being human, they come to see that each human being depends upon and is responsible for all other human beings.

Message 2: "Your home is PLANET EARTH."

It may be easier for children of the space age to fully grasp the concept of Planet Earth as home than it has been for any previous generation of humans. The first pictures of our planet as seen from the moon have been credited with significantly shifting our perspectives of ourselves and of the earth on which we live. Earth as home planet and as life-support system were made apparent in those photographs of earth, moon, astronaut, and spacecraft. Children who grow up relating to Earth as their home are comforted by the security and emboldened by the responsibility that goes with such an intimate relationship. The concept of Earth as home conveys to the young person a special relationship with all others who share that home and enhances the development of capacities central to this globally focused curriculum for the 21st century.

Message 3:
"You are a CITIZEN of _____ [your nation-state], a multicultural society.

The nation-state is a primary way in which we 21st century humans organize ourselves on planet Earth. Nationality and citizenship affect nearly all dimensions of our lives, and it is through the actions of nation-states that we deploy many resources and engage in and resolve conflicts, from the local level to the global. Inhabitants of nations have special responsibilities and opportunities to fulfill their role as citizen in locally and globally responsible ways. Because of the significance of the nation-state, a globally focused curriculum provides children with a sound foundation in understanding the role of their own and other nations within a global context.

Message 4:
"You live in an INTERRELATED WORLD."

A striking feature of the world of the 21st century is the increasing interrelatedness of human activities on a global scale. The term "interrelated" covers a range of relationships among human beings that characterize this period in history. It refers to the growing interconnectedness of the world's people through communication and transportation networks. It refers to circumstances of dependence and interdependence in which individuals, communities, and nations depend on one another, whether inequitably, as in cases of dependence, or reciprocally, as in cases of interdependence. It refers to situations in which the economic institutions of diverse nation-states are integrated on a regional level. Young children need not fully understand or recognize the various manifestations of human interrelatedness. It is critical, however, that they be aware of the vast and growing number of ways in which they and other human beings are connected. It is critical that they recognize the implications of such links for their own lives and for the potential effects of their actions on others.

■ A Call to Action

Being exposed to the concept that we are human beings living on Planet Earth as citizens of a multicultural society in an interrelated world is just the beginning. To become truly global citizens, participants in a global education must develop skills that put these thoughts into action. Students must learn about, care about, think about, choose, and act on the messages to ensure that desirable outcomes are achieved.

A global education should inspire students to learn all they can about the issues surrounding each message. Basic concepts that illuminate the messages should be a part of any global education. Knowledgeable content is the basis for exploring these messages.

Students need to be motivated to passionately care about the messages. They must internalize the concepts and values and demonstrate them in their daily lives. They must be concerned about what it means to be a human being living on this earth. They must care about the responsibilities of citizenship in our multicultural world and how our interrelatedness affects every one of us.

Knowledge and passion must be tempered by thoughtful, critical scrutiny. Students must think about the issues and the implications generated by the messages. They must reflect on their meaning in order to internalize their spirit.

Students must be encouraged to choose the messages as their own. They must acknowledge their power and believe in their efficacy. They must embrace the messages as precepts that carry with them responsibilities and challenges for the future.

Learning, caring, thinking, and choosing the messages are not sufficient goals for students of global education. Students must act on the concepts. Through their behavior they should demonstrate commitment to addressing the challenges and opportunities presented to themselves as human beings living on this planet in a multicultural society in an interrelated world.

Although simple and direct, the messages of this framework have the potential for empowering students with the necessary knowledge and will to meet the challenges of an ever-changing global world. Effective implementation of this framework as a foundation for developing integrated lessons and experiences for students will result in informed citizens who understand what is important for life in the next millennium.

3

"You are a HUMAN BEING."

■ Rationale

A curriculum grounded in a global perspective emphasizes the commonalities and connections among human beings and recognizes human differences and uniqueness. Such a species-centered perspective contrasts with a group-centered perspective that portrays humankind as a collection of culturally different, distinct, and unrelated groups. A group-centered perspective can inadvertently or purposefully encourage students to view their own culture and civilization as inherently superior to other cultures and civilizations. In contrast, a species-centered perspective emphasizes commonalities shared by all of humankind, and it encourages students to tolerate and even applaud cultural differences within the human species. Such a species-centered perspective is neither value-neutral nor value-free; rather, it promotes judgments and actions grounded in democratic principles and universal human rights extended equitably to all of humankind.

■ Outcomes

Learning Outcomes

In the culturally diverse and globally interrelated world of the 21st century, it is essential that students LEARN what it means to be a human being who lives among and depends on other human beings on Planet Earth.

Through an integrated global education, students LEARN about:

- The similarities and differences between human beings and other living things
- The ways each human being is like all other human beings
- The social nature of human beings and how this sociability affects the way we live and relate to all other human beings
- The ways human beings make and depend upon culture
- The geographical variations and historical changes in human cultures
- Oneself as a distinct member of the human species with a particular cultural heritage and individual character

1 **Students will demonstrate an understanding of the similarities and differences between human beings and other living things.**

Because we humans are only one of many millions of life forms occupying Planet Earth, one kind of knowledge children need in order to understand humankind is knowledge about similarities and differences between human beings and other living things.

An integrated global education begins in the early primary grades to develop an awareness that human beings—like all living things—experience a life cycle of birth, growth, and death and are absolutely dependent upon the earth's biosphere for food, water (hydrosphere), air (atmosphere), and protection. This awareness is expanded into deeper understandings in the later grades by examining the distinctions between life and nonlife, the biological

9

differences between humans and other life forms, and the nature of biosphere–life-form interactions.

---

2 **Students will demonstrate an understanding of the ways each human being is like all other human beings.**

We human beings are a unique species of life whose physical, emotional, and mental capabilities both set us apart from other life-forms and bring us together as a single life-form upon the earth—that is, the family of humankind. An integrated global education enables students to see themselves as members of a single species who are uniquely equipped to make and use tools; to create and learn language; to dance, sing, and celebrate life in many diverse ways; to think and make decisions; to come together in groups to support and enrich one another; to love and provide for other human beings and living things; and to use their powers for the betterment of all life on earth. An integrated global education emphasizes that one of the key distinguishing characteristics of the human species is its capacity to create culture.

---

3 **Students will demonstrate an understanding of the social nature of human beings and how this sociability affects the way we live and communicate with all other human beings.**

Human beings are social creatures who are born and live out their lives in the company of other human beings. We are members of many groups, including family, school, friendship, religious, social, cultural, and work groups. Human beings live together in communities. In focusing on the groups that are a part of the everyday lives of most children, the curriculum both engages the child and provides a sound foundation for understanding the nature of human groups generally. Children come to understand the emotional attachments that figure into group membership. Among the fundamental understandings that students develop is knowledge of the

roles and responsibilities that they and other members play within the various groups that comprise human society.

Children learn the variety of ways that groups organize themselves and the purposes that different groups serve for individuals within the group and for the larger society. For example, children learn of the variety of configurations of families both locally and globally and that human families are both alike and different the world over. They learn the ways in which group members depend upon one another, cooperate and resolve conflicts, assume responsibilities, and teach and learn from one another. They learn why all groups develop rules and the variety of ways that groups are interconnected with other groups. They also learn how to function responsibly as a member of various locally and globally interdependent groups.

---

4 **Students will demonstrate an understanding of the ways that human beings make and depend upon culture.**

Human culture, at its most basic, is the entire human-created environment. This culture spans the globe and can be seen as the interaction of four primary elements: technology, language, institutions, and beliefs. We have created and depend on these cultural elements to sustain our life on earth and to mediate our relations with other human beings and other living and nonliving things.

In developing an understanding of culture, children should recognize that technology consists of tools, plus the skill to make and use tools. Global education focuses on such mundane tools and technology as clothing, musical instruments, sports equipment, and their manufacture and use as well as such sophisticated tools and technology as satellite communication systems, nuclear plants, computers, and their manufacture and use.

Students learn that languages are systems of signs and symbols that human beings make and use to communicate ideas, information, and feelings. They become aware that human languages include more than oral and written languages. They come to understand that music, dance, and art are important forms of human language.

Institutions are defined as human beings' enduring creations for meeting certain basic recurring social needs. Students begin to develop an understanding of the basic human institutions of family, government, economics, education, and religion.

An integrated global education helps children see beliefs as a central element of culture and understand that all human beings hold beliefs about what is true; about what is good or bad, right or wrong; and about what is beautiful or ugly, attractive or unattractive.

5 **Students will demonstrate an understanding of geographical variations and historical changes in human cultures.**

Although all human beings create culture, human culture is not the same the world over. Global education provides students with an awareness and basic knowledge of geographical variations in culture. Children come to see how different groups in different parts of the world are similar and different in their technology, languages, institutions, and beliefs. Students begin to understand that the rich cultural diversity that exists around the globe is a result of human beings adapting to the natural environment and engaging in the processes of cultural invention and diffusion. They learn that the culture shared by any group of human beings is constantly changing as conditions in any given location change, as group members move, and as groups with different cultural patterns come into contact with one another.

6 **Students will demonstrate an understanding of themselves as distinct members of the human species with a particular cultural heritage and individual character.**

A sound global education provides each child with accurate and complete information about herself or himself that is conveyed in self-affirming and self-respecting ways. It develops children's understanding of and respect for their own personal heritages and histories. Such self-focused knowledge development is always approached from a global perspective—that is, in ways that help children see how they are linked to all other human beings who share Planet Earth as their home and who have rights and responsibilities as citizens who are empowered and entrusted to care, think, choose, and act for the common good.

Caring Outcomes

The ability to care enables people to relate effectively to others. The concept of "relating effectively to others" means being able to develop friendships, work with other people, and communicate, but it also means much more. It encompasses the ability to understand, appreciate, and recognize as legitimate the wide range of human experiences—current, past, and future—around the planet. Caring is enhanced through the growth of perceptions and orientations that enable people to escape from rigid, restricted perspectives to more flexible, open perspectives grounded in a commitment to human dignity and universal human rights.

Through an integrated global education, students' capacity to CARE is enhanced by:

- Self-awareness

- Self-esteem and a sense of efficacy

- Consciousness of perspective

- Empathy

- Altruism

- Avoidance of stereotyping

- Growing beyond egocentric and ethnocentric perspectives

1 Students will demonstrate an understanding of self, including recognizing strengths and compensating for weaknesses.

Self-awareness rooted in a global perspective enables young people to see themselves as human beings, whose home is Planet Earth, who are citizens of a multicultural society, living in an interrelated world, and who learn, care, think, choose, and act to celebrate life on this planet and to meet the global challenges confronting humankind. Each of the following caring capacities both rests upon and enhances self-awareness.

2 Students will exhibit self-esteem and demonstrate belief in their ability to make a difference.

The capacity to care, think, choose, and act rests ultimately upon a person's self-esteem and sense of efficacy. Political socialization research has consistently affirmed that this kind of self-perception is fundamental to active citizenship. If people feel worthless and ineffective, they perceive that there is nothing to be gained by becoming involved. If, on the other hand, people feel confident and efficacious, involvement follows.

Self-esteem cannot be "taught." Rather, it flourishes or withers depending on the environment or climate in which a child grows. Schools that respond to the needs of the individual child and provide opportunities for all children to be responsible, participating citizens of the school community are fostering self-esteem and efficacy.

A critical element of school climate is the content of the curriculum and the manner in which it is presented. The cultural and ethnic diversity of society and the diversity of humankind should be presented in a positive way, so that children from a broad range of backgrounds and heritages can proudly identify with the people they find in their studies.

3 Students will demonstrate an understanding, appreciation, and recognition of the wide range of human experiences and perspectives.

Perspective consciousness is a key underlying competence associated with the development of a global perspective. It is closely related to the capacity to empathize and to decreased egocentrism and ethnocentrism. The recognition of perspective is the first step toward internalizing the fact that the reality one person experiences is not necessarily the reality that other people experience. As such, it goes far beyond opinion and is the basis for understanding and respecting both cultural and individual differences.

Perspective consciousness is extended when students recognize that their own view of the world is not universally shared, and when they recognize that this view has been, and continues to be, shaped by influences that often escape conscious detection. The more students are able to project themselves into alternative perspectives, the more their consciousness is extended.

4 Students will demonstrate empathy by recognizing and understanding others' needs, feelings, and interests.

Empathy is the capacity to "step into another's shoes" and, accordingly, perceive the world as others perceive it. It is the ability to sympathetically imagine how an action, institution, or event appears to persons in a different social or situational context.

Increasing the ability to empathize involves being able to describe accurately the thoughts and feelings of others. Being able to explain why one might think, feel, or act the same way as another if one were in the other's social and situational setting is an indication of empathy.

5 Students will demonstrate a sense of altruism through interaction with others.

Altruism goes beyond empathy. It is the capacity to not only want to bring about something good for another, but to actually do it, often at some cost to one's self. Increasing the capacity for altruism involves valuing and respecting other human beings and seeing how the welfare of others is linked to one's own welfare. It includes viewing all human beings as connected to one another and having a long-range perspective on achieving the general good. Being able to carry out projects for achieving the general good and having imagination and the willingness to take risks are indicators of this capacity.

6 Students will demonstrate an understanding of stereotypes and avoid their use in word and deed.

Stereotyping is the use of universal and closed generalizations about or characterizations of a group, process, social institution, society, or ideology. There are three main reasons for breaking down stereotypes:

- They are not true. Exceptions to every universal and closed generalization or characterization can be found.

- They can cause trouble. Stereotypes are beliefs, and since people act or behave according to what they believe, stereotypes (since they are not true!) can cause trouble.

- They hurt. Many stereotypes cut to the quick of the human psyche and cripple human capacities. Children who hold stereotypic perceptions harm not only other people but themselves. Stereotyping limits associations with others and closes opportunities for cooperation and collaboration. Ultimately, stereotypic thinking is the basis for racist institutions and societies.

Growing beyond stereotypic perceptions involves developing awareness of the inaccuracy and danger inherent in any generalized statements. Students can transcend stereotypic thinking by avoiding negative characterizations of groups, recognizing the egocentric and ethnocentric basis for stereotypes, and examining who is advantaged by stereotypic perceptions.

7 Students will demonstrate growth beyond egocentric perceptions by being receptive to new ideas and communicating effectively with others.

Egocentric perception is the assumption that one's "view of the world" is the only view and, thus, the right view. It is also the unconscious assumption that one is the center of the universe and that others share this perception. When others fail to share this assumption, they may be judged morally deficient and undeserving of respect and concern. People with egocentric perceptions see enhancement of their own narrow interests as the sole criterion for deciding what is good.

Growing beyond egocentric perceptions involves recognizing the existence of multiple perspectives (both physical and sociopsychological) and being able to project oneself into alternative perspectives. It includes accepting alternative perspectives as legitimate explanations for differences of opinion and being able to value equally others' and one's own self-interests. Considering and acting in response to the interests and welfare of others indicates that one has overcome egocentric perceptions.

8 Students will demonstrate growth beyond ethnocentric perceptions by being receptive to new ideas and communicating effectively with others.

Ethnocentric perceptions are similar to egocentric perceptions. Whereas egocentricity involves one's relationships to individuals, ethnocentricity involves

13

one's relationship to groups. Ethnocentric perception is the view that one's own group is the center of everything. The individual tends to think of the actions, customs, institutions, and ideologies of the groups to which she or he belongs as superior to the actions and beliefs of outside groups. Such a person uses the enhancement of her or his own group's narrow and short-range interests as the sole criterion for deciding what is good.

Growing beyond ethnocentric perceptions involves recognizing that one's own and others' group affiliations (family, community, nation, and so on) shape individual perspectives. It means balancing allegiance to one's own groups with the capacity to respect and to relate effectively to other groups. Being able to relate to other groups without judging them and being able to consider and act in response to the interest and welfare of other groups in addition to one's own are indicators of growth.

Thinking Outcomes

As we move into the information age, the ability to critically analyze the voluminous amount of data available becomes increasingly important. Technology is making it possible for information to be transmitted by anyone, anywhere, at any time. Without the ability to think carefully and to apply cognitive skills appropriately, students are hampered in making independent decisions. Misinformation about other human beings and societies is rampant and can undermine the intent of a message if not countered by the development of thinking skills.

Through an integrated global education, students THINK about:

- Why human beings behave the way they do

- What questions will help them understand what it means to be human

- What is fact and what is opinion

1 Students will demonstrate an understanding of why human beings behave the way they do.

To be able to learn and care about themselves and others as human beings, students need to develop the ability to identify the causes and effects of actions. An integrated global education stresses the importance of developing the ability to identify the reasons people act the way they do and the results of their actions. Students must also think about their own actions and the consequences of their deeds on others and the environment.

2 Students will ask questions that demonstrate the need to understand human beings and their actions.

Knowing the questions to ask that will elicit correct information about others is imperative. Questions that probe, seek clarification, and determine the speaker's motivation must be a part of each student's mental schema in evaluating data. Such an approach provides the skills needed to discern stereotypical comments and validate perceptions about themselves and others.

An integrated global curriculum develops questioning skills at every opportunity. Questions about ourselves, others, cultures, societies, history, and so on, are encouraged and modeled for students. Through an open and thoughtful exchange of information and ideas, the concept of humanness is expanded and strengthened.

3 Students will demonstrate an understanding of the differences between what is fact and what is opinion.

Understanding multiple perspectives and avoiding stereotyping requires the ability to distinguish between fact and opinion. Thinking skills that increase students' capacity for identifying what is true and what reflects bias or inaccurate interpretations are critical for global citizens. It is too easy for prejudice to masquerade as truth and intercept the message that we are all human beings.

Knowledge without thinking leads to premature decisions and uncritical acceptance of the ideas and perceptions of others. Thinking about being human and all its ramifications is a powerful first step in global education.

Choosing Outcomes

Embracing the concept of what it means to be human prompts students to make choices. Students should choose to take actions that provide them with accurate information, that demonstrate their caring about other humans, that show their internalization of thinking about what it means to be a human being.

Through an integrated global education, students CHOOSE:

- To see others' point of view
- To seek additional information
- To find alternatives to situations that allow everyone to "win"

1 **Students will demonstrate an understanding of others' points of view through using and evaluating appropriate skills of observation, perspective taking, reasoning, problem solving, and decision making.**

Choosing to see another's point of view requires an appreciation for diversity and a welcoming of the opportunities offered by a multitude of perspectives. It also means understanding that diversity can pose potential conflict. To understand the positions of others and to be prepared to deal with differences requires the ability to reason and solve problems. It requires choosing to view situations from different perspectives. It requires the skill of observing that differences exist and identifying what those differences are.

2 **Students will seek additional information about themselves, others, and the situation before making decisions.**

Students who understand what it means to be human and who appreciate others will choose to seek additional information before making decisions. They will understand that there are reasons and explanations for the actions of people that are not always readily apparent. They will choose to look beyond the obvious to see from another's perspective before taking action.

Students with a global perspective will approach decision making in a systemic way. After identification of a problem, they will identify key stakeholders in the situation and involve as many as possible in learning about the situation and in generating solutions. They will strive for consensus among the stakeholders to achieve a shared vision of the ideal. They will use this consensual vision to identify specific, concrete actions to be taken and the resources needed to achieve and maintain the ideal state. Obtaining commitment, building action plans, and implementing these plans naturally follow.

3 **Students will demonstrate the ability to find alternatives to situations that allow everyone to "win."**

Empathy and acceptance of others will prompt students to design solutions to problems that take into account the needs and feelings of all involved. They will choose to incorporate the ideas, requirements, and opinions of others in determining resolutions to problems. They will understand that basic concerns and complex global problems require cooperation to achieve solutions. The importance of preserving self and others will be paramount in their considerations.

Acting Outcomes

Students who understand what it means to be a human being act to improve the human condition, having confidence in themselves and their own and others' capacities to make a difference. They realize that human beings have a responsibility to take actions that benefit mankind.

Through an integrated global education, children ACT by:

- Showing respect for other human beings
- Being sensitive to others
- Obtaining information about others
- Actively seeking opportunities to interact with people who are different from themselves

1 Students will demonstrate respect for themselves and other human beings.

We show respect for other human beings by treating others as we would like to be treated. Respect includes listening with attention and accepting the opinions of others. Respect begins with appreciating ourselves and believing that we are important. This respect is extended to those around us, both adults and other children, when we give consideration to their positions. Global respect is evident when we accept others, regardless of country, social condition, ethnicity, and so on, as human beings with feelings and thoughts as valid as our own.

2 Students will demonstrate sensitivity to others and an understanding that to be different is neither better nor worse.

We exhibit sensitivity by understanding the feelings of other people. Classroom projects that focus on the needs of others around the world help children to develop a global sensitivity. Our behavior toward those around us reflects our ability to apply this action to others far removed.

3 Students will actively obtain information about others to inform their decisions and to understand the context of other people.

Seeking information about others is evidence of a global perspective. Children who are aware of themselves and others desire to know more. They see similarities and differences and pursue knowledge that will augment what they know. They initiate an interest in others in conversation and assignments. They ask questions to augment their knowledge and inform their actions.

4 Students will demonstrate acceptance of others by actively seeking opportunities to interact with people who are different.

A global education instills in its recipients a desire to work and play with other human beings. Diversity is seen as valuable and a strength. This positive view is exhibited in the way students form groups, choose partners, welcome newcomers. Differences among people are celebrated and viewed as opportunities for growth.

4

"Your home is PLANET EARTH."

■ Rationale

All life forms are dependent on the life-support systems of Planet Earth. Children must develop a relationship with the earth that is based on an understanding of the planet as their home and a realization of their responsibility for that home. Their actions and decisions must be tempered by their understanding and acceptance of this intimate relationship. The life–sustaining nature of Planet Earth is not a given. It is only through conscientious and wise stewardship that life will continue to flourish.

■ Outcomes

Learning Outcomes

In the culturally diverse and globally interdependent world of the 21st century, it is essential for students to recognize their dependence upon Planet Earth, their place in the natural environment of the planet, and their relationship to other living things with whom they share the earth.

Through an integrated global education, children LEARN about:

- The place of Planet Earth in the universe
- The ecosystem of Planet Earth
- Human-ecosystem relationships
- The earth's cultural geography
- The geographical/physical features of one's own community and country and their place among others on Planet Earth in the 21st century

1 Students will demonstrate an understanding about the place of Planet Earth in the universe.

Global education introduces children to historical changes in the ways people around the world have viewed the shape and location of the earth. It provides children with a basic understanding of the relationship between earth and sun, particularly as it concerns day and night and seasonal changes. Children become aware of the location of the earth in the solar system, the solar system in the galaxy, and the galaxy in the universe. Global education also explores the cultural significance and public controversy surrounding space exploration and examines the scientific research and speculation about the existence of life elsewhere in the universe.

2 Students will demonstrate an understanding of the ecosystem of Planet Earth.

An integrated global education lays the foundation for an understanding of the earth's biosphere and the energy resources that support human life. Included in such an understanding is knowledge about the planet's physical features. Careful attention is given to developing children's understanding that the biosphere is an ecosystem composed of systems within systems. Children learn how different kinds of maps, globes, and diagrams can be used to learn about and to describe the planet's physical geography; how math can be used to measure and count various aspects of the physical features of the earth; and how literature and the arts can describe and communicate people's perceptions of earth's physical features.

3 Students will demonstrate an understanding of human-ecosystem relationships.

An education based in a global perspective reveals human beings as an integral part of the planetwide ecosystem. Such a perspective highlights at least four things about the relationships between humans and the natural environment: (1) the dependence of humankind upon resources found in nature; (2) the limited and finite characteristics of many natural resources; (3) the global nature of the planet's ecosystem; and (4) the importance of developing human life-styles and technologies that support and maintain a regenerative, life-sustaining ecosystem.

Children explore the consequences of human actions on the natural environment and are sensitized to the potential ramifications of such actions. They examine cultural differences in relating to the natural environment throughout history and around the world and are introduced to diverse beliefs about appropriate relations between human beings and the earth/nature. Global education illuminates the many diverse and creative ways human beings express their feelings for and relationships to their natural environment through literature and the arts.

4 Students will demonstrate an understanding of the earth's cultural geography.

Children need basic understanding of the cultural geography of their community and country, including where other communities and cities are located and where different cultural, social, economic, and political activities are carried out. Important knowledge about cultural geography—how human beings use and interact with the physical environment—is introduced in the early grades through the exploration of space use in schools and homes and land use in communities. In the upper grades, global education introduces children to spatial variations in human culture. This study includes developing basic understanding of where cultural groups are located on the face of the globe and the differing ways cultural groups use space.

Examining migration patterns within students' own nation and throughout the world, patterns of population growth and urban growth, and the social problems associated with migration and urbanization are important features of a global education. An especially prominent focus for global education is an introduction to indigenous peoples and to the global diaspora of diverse cultural groups throughout human history.

5 Students will demonstrate an understanding of the geographical and physical features of their own community and country and their place among others on Planet Earth in the 21st century.

A sound foundation of information about one's own community and country is critical to effective participation in the globally interdependent world of the 21st century. Children should know the location of their community and country on Planet Earth and the space they encompass, and they should be able to identify and locate other countries on the globe. Students should also have a basic understanding of their community's and country's physical and geographical features, and they should understand how natural resources are used and how the resources themselves are affected by this use.

Caring Outcomes

In caring for Planet Earth as their home, children will feel a sense of efficacy in their own and others' potential to maintain or renew a life–supporting, enriching ecosystem. They will embrace the responsibility of being stewards of the earth, caring about the planet and how the deeds of each person affect it.

Through an integrated global education, children CARE about:

- Understanding and evaluating their own effect on the earth

- Accepting responsibility for their own and others' effect on the earth

- Demonstrating stewardship of the earth by recognizing and protecting the delicate balance of the planet's life–support system

1 Students will demonstrate an understanding of and be able to evaluate their individual effect on Planet Earth.

Global education promotes in students a feeling of responsibility for maintaining the system of Planet Earth. Students realize that the actions of each individual affect the earth for better or for worse. Students begin to see that their actions do matter and affect the system as a whole. They see the interrelatedness of every action and take care to ensure that their actions have a positive effect.

2 Students will accept responsibility for their individual actions.

An understanding of how individual deeds affect the system leads to the acceptance of responsibility for these actions. Global education instills in students a feeling of obligation to Planet Earth that leads them to evaluate the effect of all activities on the various subsystems of the planet. Students realize that this obligation is both an individual and a group responsibility. Everyone is charged with caring for the earth.

3 Students will demonstrate stewardship of the earth.

Students care about the earth by demonstrating through word and deed their stewardship of the planet. Students understand the delicate balance that exists among the life forms of the earth and behave accordingly. Their actions are filtered through a lens showing their effect on the earth's subsystems. They strive to preserve and enhance the balance that nature has established. This care is evidenced

through conservation of resources, respect for the natural cycles in nature, and an understanding of how actions today effect the life of tomorrow.

Thinking Outcomes

The development and refinement of thinking skills is a central part of global education. Global education teaches students the importance of thinking about the environment, and it encourages them to use their reasoning skills to make decisions that will affect the earth in a positive way.

Through an integrated global education, children THINK about:

- The differences between fact and opinion
- Solving problems by asking questions and evaluating responses
- The cause and effect of actions on the system of Planet Earth

1 Students will demonstrate an understanding of the differences between fact and opinion.

Erroneous or insufficient information can result in actions that harm the earth and its life forms. Global education encourages students to differentiate between fact and opinion so as to make informed decisions that have a positive effect on the planet. Students learn that actions based on opinion rather than fact can be disastrous.

2 Students will solve problems by asking questions and evaluating responses.

Students will learn to analyze all information available so as to make informed decisions. They will be able to identify relevant facts, synthesize data from numerous sources, and develop rationales for actions that are not injurious to the planet. From a very young age, human beings ask questions, and

19

throughout our lifetime, we continue to ask questions. Our individual and collective ability to formulate clear and accurate pictures of the world around us rests, in large measure, on our capacity for asking questions and evaluating the responses we receive. Increased competency in asking questions and evaluating responses involves a growing capacity to frame productive questions and to identify the best person(s) or other source(s) to answer a given question. As students gain experience, they will be able to select effective ways to communicate questions (e.g., write a letter, use the telephone, conduct an interview, develop a survey). Over time, they will develop the ability to evaluate the sufficiency and veracity of the answers received to answer the questions asked.

3 Students will demonstrate an understanding of the cause and effect of actions on the system of Planet Earth.

Being constantly aware of the causes and effects of actions and decisions provides students with the ability to maintain the balance of life found on Planet Earth. Children who think about how their deeds affect both their immediate world and the larger world around them make better judgements and ensure that the planet is preserved and enhanced. Children who think about the environment look beyond surface appearances to the underlying causes of problems. They also think about both the immediate and long–term effects of actions.

Choosing Outcomes

Children who embrace the principles of global education cherish the life of Planet Earth in all its myriad forms. They choose to take actions that demonstrate their regard for life and they apply scientific methods to gather information in support of their commitment. They realize that choices have to be made and they base their choices on the best information available and on their respect for the

environment.

Through an integrated global education, children CHOOSE to:

- Involve themselves as amateur scientists in scientific inquiry, arriving at their own conclusions
- Make decisions that respect the Planet Earth and all its life forms
- Seek information from a variety of disciplines in their study of the earth: history, geography, art, music, science, language, math, and literature

1 Students will use scientific methods to obtain information.

Students of global education understand the benefits of scientific inquiry and choose to use this method to increase their knowledge about the planet and how it functions. Practice in generating and testing hypotheses helps children avoid the pitfalls of centering on only one or a limited number of possible explanations for any situation. Growing competencies in hypothesizing include formulating hypotheses on the basis of evidence and making rational arguments as to the legitimacy of the evidence cited. Identifying alternative ways of testing a hypothesis and selecting and justifying the best means of testing a hypothesis are also evidence of this ability.

Students pose questions, develop hypotheses, conduct experiments, and learn from the results. They believe knowledge will enhance their ability to preserve the earth and its life forms.

2 Students will make decisions that respect the Planet Earth.

Children use their knowledge and the results of their scientific inquiries to make decisions that show respect for the planet and its life forms. They choose to keep informed and use their understandings to make decisions that benefit the earth and its life forms. They choose to make maintaining the balance of nature a primary consideration in their lives.

Global education instills in students a desire to improve and maintain the environment. Children choose to have a positive effect on other people and the world around them. They make a conscious choice to enhance the environment through deeds and words that manifest this concern.

3 Students use information from various disciplines to inform their decisions.

Global education makes students realize the interconnectedness of life and the complexities of Planet Earth's problems. Students choose to bring knowledge from all disciplines to bear on problems in order to implement decisions that take into account this interrelatedness of life. They understand that all subjects have much wisdom to contribute to the challenge of earth's effective and efficient functioning. They understand that no one discipline has the answers.

Acting Outcomes

Civic participation is an important avenue through which concern for the planet can be demonstrated. By working with our fellow human beings, we will find solutions for the problems facing the planet in the 21st century. But our actions must reflect an understanding of the intricacies of the earth's many subsystems if we are to maintain the safety of the planet.

Through an integrated global education, children ACT:

- In cooperation and collaboration with others to maintain the balance of life in the system of Planet Earth

- By participating in civic activities that demonstrate an understanding and appreciation for the complexity of the earth's system

- With the understanding that the environment is a closed system

1 Students will cooperate with others to maintain the balance of life.

Global education encourages students to work with others to ensure the continuation of Planet Earth. Joint action is seen as a necessary and an important method for dealing with the many interrelated problems confronting life on earth. Though individual commitment to preserving earth is necessary, the combined efforts of many are called for to combat the problems that everyone faces.

2 Students will participate in civic activities.

Global education promotes participation in civic activities. Active engagement with governmental processes is an effective way to make others aware of the importance of preserving the delicate balance of life on Planet Earth and to persuade others of the need for cooperative action. The system of Planet Earth is a complex one, and responsibility for the earth belongs to everyone. Action based on accurate information is the key to maintaining the earth's system.

3 Students will demonstrate an understanding of the environment as a closed system.

Effective actions to preserve the environment and all its life forms requires an understanding of the earth as a closed system. This system has a finite number of natural resources that are unequally distributed or economically unavailable to many. Global education teaches students to evaluate world conditions, analyze data, and make decisions based on facts. Global education also advocates the implementation of decisions based on the goal of honoring Planet Earth.

5

"You are a CITIZEN of _____ [your nation–state] _____, a multicultural society."

■ Rationale

Nationality and citizenship are significant factors in the lives of all human beings. Nation-states decide how many resources are deployed. Nation–states also resolve local and global conflicts. Citizens of nations have responsibilities on both local and global levels. A global curriculum provides children with a sound foundation and context for exercising their roles as citizens of their own nation within a global context.

■ Outcomes

In the culturally diverse and globally interrelated world of the 21st century, it is essential that students LEARN what it means to be citizens of their own nation. Children should learn about the social, cultural, and political heritage of their nation and the people, natural environment, and culture of contemporary nations.

Through an integrated global education, students LEARN about:

• The historical development of their nation, the people of the nation, the experiences and contributions of diverse ethnic groups, and the emerging ethnic/cultural profile of the population

• The geographical features and natural environment of the nation and human-environmental interactions

• The civic culture of the nation and the principles on which the nation is founded

• Their own communities within the larger contexts of the nation and world

1 **Students will demonstrate knowledge about the historical development of their nation, the people of the nation, the experiences and contributions of diverse ethnic groups, and the emerging ethnic/cultural profile of the population.**

The social history of most nations on earth is rich in stories of peoples of diverse heritages and backgrounds. This history told from a global perspective highlights the interrelationship of the cultural diversity of the population of the nation and global events and conditions. To prepare children to understand the contemporary society in which they live, the history of their nation is told not as one story beginning with the "founding" of the nation, but as many stories of all the peoples who figured in its prehistory, creation, and unfolding development. The major events and eras in the nation's history are told not as stories of isolated events and one–dimensional actors, but as events unfolding in global contexts shaped by multidimensional actors representing diverse groups.

Children study the indigenous peoples of the land as well as the various immigrant groups who figure in the nation's history. They develop a growing appreciation for the ways that each historical time and setting affects "the immigrant experience" and shapes how each immigrant group responds to becoming members of this society. They begin to understand some of the ways that the changing ethnic and cultural make-up of the population may affect society in the 21st century. They develop a growing understanding of the sources of tensions that arise among diverse ethnic/cultural groups and the conditions that reduce such tensions and bring people together.

They recognize that people from disparate backgrounds and cultural heritages have similar aspirations that bring them to a specific place. They also recognize how these commonly held aspirations help forge a nation based on common goals. Students are introduced to individuals from many different heritages and economic circumstances who have been instrumental in solving social problems and shaping the character of their nation. They come to see the role that vision, planning, collaboration, and enduring commitment play in achieving better social conditions for all people.

2 Students will demonstrate an understanding of the geographical features and natural environment of the nation and human-environmental interactions.

The concept of the global ecosystem is foundational to the exploration of the geographical features and natural environment of every nation on the planet. One of the most important understandings conveyed to children is that the natural environment of any nation is a part of the global ecosystem and that political boundaries do not define and cannot contain environmental boundaries. Children anchor this understanding in basic knowledge about the nature and location of the physical features of the landscape and the character and distribution of natural resources. They examine and establish criteria for evaluating alternative uses of natural resources, setting this exploration in a global context that considers such issues as equity of access for humankind and the stability of the ecosystem.

3 Students will demonstrate an understanding of the civic culture of the nation and the principles on which the nation is founded.

Civic culture is the public sphere where issues relating to the identification, selection, and distribution of the public resources are addressed and resolved. It is both the right and the responsibility of all citizens to be active participants in the civic culture of their society. Global interdependence and cultural diversity continually expand the culture of society. Young people who are receiving a quality education for the 21st century learn about the founding of their nation and the values on which it rests. They learn about the undergirding principles and the governmental structures supporting the country's principles and they study the struggles for justice, liberty, and equity of different groups throughout the nation's history. They learn that human values are shared by human beings around the globe.

4 Students will demonstrate an understanding of their own communities within the larger contexts of region, nation, and world.

The education of young children has traditionally begun with investigations of their immediate communities. Children need to understand that communities are networks of interdependent individuals and groups. Children need to learn to identify and describe the functions of cultural, social, religious, governmental, economic, and educational institutions within their own communities and to see the similarities and differences between these and other such institutions in communities throughout the world. As the 21st century comes into view, those local communities are becoming potent laboratories for learning about the world. The world impinges upon the people and events in every community and they in turn impinge upon the world far beyond the local setting. A quality global education helps children gain an awareness of how the cultural, social, religious, governmental, economic, and educational institutions within their own communities relate with other communities throughout the state, the nation, and even the world to provide the goods and services to meet the needs of local residents. Children develop some familiarity with differences in types of communities in which people live—urban, suburban, and rural—and how communities change over time.

Caring Outcomes

Citizens of the 21st century care about both their immediate social structure and the larger global societies to which everyone belongs. This caring is reflected in an understanding of a citizen's roles and responsibilities in an interrelated world. Citizens care about relationships and realize that these relationships are intricate and intertwined, spanning systems from all nations.

In an integrated global education, children CARE about:

- Their roles and responsibilities as citizens in interrelated local, national, and global groups and contexts
- Other nations, their governments, and peoples around the globe and how these are related to and compare with their own nation

1 Students will demonstrate an understanding of a citizen's roles and responsibilities in interrelated local, national, and global groups and contexts.

An education grounded in a global perspective is committed to providing children with well-defined conceptual maps of the many alternative routes to civic action that are open to them as a result of the growing numbers of interrelated global systems that cut across and through local, state, national, and global groups and contexts. Children learn that the choices they make regarding the consumption of resources within their local communities have the potential to affect not only themselves and their community, but people throughout the world. They develop the habit of thinking globally when acting locally as they trace the effects of their actions through ever more complex webs of interaction. They learn to generate moral and ethical standards by which to judge action and social policy as they practice civically responsible decision making and action taking.

2 Students will demonstrate knowledge about other nations, their governments, and people around the globe and how these are related to and compare with their own nation.

Children are introduced to the various forms of governments devised by different peoples throughout history and around the world. They are introduced to the theories behind diverse governmental structures and compare the theories with the actual governments that have grown out of the theories. They see the relationship between the values held by government leaders and the governmental structures and processes that develop. They begin to recognize that some governments are more responsible and effective than others in providing for the welfare of their citizens and in participating in the international community. They study examples of citizens rejecting their government regimes and building more responsive governments. They learn of the major international alliances that their nation has formed with other nations to address human problems such as national security and environmental destruction, and they are able to recognize the types of problems and issues that are more effectively addressed through multinational cooperation.

Thinking Outcomes

Higher order thinking skills become increasingly important as students confront the dilemmas of the 21st century. Problems are more complex and require the ability to apply critical analysis and inquiry skills in the problem–solving process. They require that children be able to make inferences based on sound evidence. Global problems are important to everyone, and every citizen has the responsibility to both think about global issues and work to resolve them.

In an integrated global education, children THINK about:

- Analyzing and evaluating world issues
- Making inferences based on sound evidence

1 Students will demonstrate the ability to analyze and evaluate world issues.

Global challenges and opportunities confront us all. They can be categorized under the headings of environment, health and well-being, human rights, and violence and conflict. Young people who master the knowledge, skills, and capacities outlined in this framework can be expected to handle developmentally appropriate versions of the identified global challenges and opportunities. For example, the child who applies the principles of fairness in classroom rule making and enforcement is preparing for adult responsibilities and challenges.

These global challenges and opportunities include many issues that require analysis and evaluation. Assuring human rights encompasses issues of freedom, of entitlements, and of responsibilities. Improving and maintaining the quality of the environment prompts discussion of resource consumption and technological impact. Improving and maintaining health and well-being necessitates analysis of hunger, housing, education, drugs, poverty, the growing economic gap between rich and poor. Reducing violence and conflict is in some way part of the life of all students; for instance, they must confront the violence of nature (floods, hurricanes, tornadoes, drought, earthquakes), the violence of machines (weapons, factories, air and ground traffic accidents), and the violence of people (terrorism, gangs, crime).

2 Students will demonstrate the ability to make inferences are based on sound evidence.

The act of inferring is going beyond information that is displayed and looking for ideas that are implicit. Children develop their skills of inferring when they distinguish explicitly present information from inferences and distinguish soundly based inferences from those not so firmly grounded in evidence. Children make sound inferences when they use logic, identifying and justifying the evidence on which their inferences are based.

Choosing Outcomes

Citizens of multicultural societies are conscientious about how they make decisions, being careful to consider their responsibilities to a global world. They choose to use their abilities to make meaning from their knowledge and experiences that are based on a global perspective. They use their imaginations to envision alternatives that have beneficial results for other nations as well as their own. They choose to use their abilities not in a parochial manner, but in an open–minded manner.

In an integrated global education, children CHOOSE to:

- Make decisions that reflect thoughtfulness and an understanding of their responsibilities as citizens
- Construct meaning from knowledge and experience
- Use their imaginations to envision alternatives that benefit all humans

1 Students will make decisions that reflect thoughtfulness and an understanding of their responsibilities as citizens.

Decision making is the process of choosing among two or more alternatives. Competent decision making begins with recognizing when a decision is called for, when there is a choice to be made. Global education seeks to develop citizens who are ever alert to such occasions, who exercise their decision-making skills as active participants in civic processes, who can trace the ramifications of their decisions or actions beyond immediate local impacts to global and future impacts, who are ethical and moral decision makers, and who hold their public officials to the same standards. The more competent and confident students are in their capacities to make good decisions, the greater the likelihood that they will be active and effective participants in civic decision making.

2 Students will construct meaning from knowledge and experience.

Human beings are meaning makers; that is, we link the information we take in to the conceptual maps we already have in an attempt to make sense of the new information. In the process, we expand and change existing concepts to accommodate the new information. The skill of conceptualizing—or meaning making—requires both comparing and classifying and involves the two interrelated processes of analyzing and synthesizing. The ability to break larger, more inclusive concepts into subconcepts (analysis) and the ability to combine objects, experiences, and ideas into larger, more inclusive concepts (synthesis) are both evidence of children's growing competence in making meaning.

3 Students will use their imaginations to envision alternatives that benefit all humans.

The capacity to imagine alternative realities is becoming an increasingly important skill for human survival. It is related to both the capacity for perspective taking and to an understanding of the interconnectedness of the human species and the life-support systems of the planet. Growing competencies in imagining include projecting oneself into alternative life situations through time and space. This ability includes being able to visualize alternative pasts or past events and to identify changes in present conditions that would grow out of the alternative past; it also includes being able to imagine the future. Being able to recognize the ramifications of every projected change (past, present, future) makes possible the generation of alternative futures, which in turn allow students to establish criteria for evaluating the desirability of each, make choices based on the criteria, and develop strategies for achieving them.

Acting Outcomes

The opportunities for action as a citizen in a multicultural society are many. Civic responsibility and the need for action can be developed in students at an early age. From participation in school assignments to participation in projects sponsored by groups outside of the school structure, children have many opportunities to practice and exhibit the principles of civic duty.

In an integrated global education, students ACT by:

- Participating in the civic processes of their society
- Cooperating with others for the good of all societies
- Making decisions using consensus processes
- Communicating with others

1 Students will participate in the civic processes of their society.

From the earliest grades, children need opportunities to practice their citizenship skills by taking part in group decision making and problem solving in the social groups to which they belong. Teachers who, from the earliest grades, involve children in establishing and enforcing classroom rules are promoting increased civic competence. This competence is reinforced and extended as students participate in schoolwide student government activities and work with local governmental structures to solve such community problems as safe pedestrian routes or parks to accommodate all age groups. The more opportunities that children have to apply their knowledge, skills, and caring capacities in solving real-life social problems, the more competent and confident citizens they become.

2 Students will cooperate with others for the good of all societies.

Simulated problem–solving and decision-making exercises are valuable learning experiences that become even more valuable when they are enriched by real-life experiences in working through social issues in classrooms, schools, neighborhoods, and communities. As in real–life situations, these simulations and exercises are most beneficial when designed for group interactions. Problems confronting societies in this and future centuries are intricate and will depend on the cooperation of many different peoples to solve. Only by working together for the good of all will we devise solutions for the problems confronting us all.

3 Students will make decisions using consensus processes.

Global education develops students' capacities for both individual and group decision making. It recognizes that sound decisions rest on a firm foundation of knowledge and skills. In making decisions, students identify the need for a decision, generate alternative actions that could be taken, and think about the values to be considered in assessing alternatives. They identify and gather the information needed to determine the possible consequences of each alternative, assess both the potential negative and positive consequences of pursuing each alternative, and trace those consequences into the future. Students use consensus to evaluate each consequence in light of the values established, rank and prioritize the possibilities, and then reach a decision. They are prepared to communicate to others their justifications for the decision and are open to changing any decision if new information or changed conditions warrant doing so.

4 Students will communicate with others.

Communicating with others is more than speaking effectively and using other communication arts. It also involves determining what information needs to be communicated and choosing the best media to use. It means targeting the appropriate audience and crafting the information in a way that will influence this audience. An important part of communicating is choosing the timing and conditions that will enable a particular message to have the greatest effect.

6

"You live in an INTERRELATED WORLD."

■ Rationale

The 21st century will be characterized by the interrelatedness of human activities on a global scale. Both individuals and groups of people will be involved in multiple interrelated relationships. Communication and transportation networks will allow individuals and nations to work together regardless of their geographic location. This interconnectedness also means that conflicts will affect people far from the areas of conflict. It is important that young children begin to appreciate this human interrelatedness. They must see their connection to the larger world around them.

■ Outcomes

Learning Outcomes

In the culturally diverse and globally interrelated world of the 21st century, it is essential for students to understand the many ways in which the peoples of the world are linked to one another.

Through an integrated global education, students LEARN about:

- The many ways peoples and nations are linked in an interrelated global system
- How the many dimensions of this global interrelatedness developed over time
- How these global links affect their role as citizens of one nation among other nations
- The importance of increasing opportunities for interaction among people

1 **Students will demonstrate an understanding of the many ways peoples and nations are linked in an interrelated global system.**

Children who will live out their adult lives in the 21st century need conceptual maps that portray the world as a complex of overlapping and diverse connections, networks, and systems. A quality education based in the realities of the 21st century provides opportunities to explore these connections both within national borders and throughout the world. Children learn that the local and global links connecting human beings are many and diverse and have differing degrees and kinds of effects on people's lives. Such local and global links range from the technological links of communication and transportation to the more abstract political and cultural links of international governmental organizations (e.g., the United Nations) and cross-national nongovernmental organizations (e.g., the Girl Scouts). Children who learn to "see" such linkages will be better prepared to curtail potentially destructive links and to promote and capitalize on links that have the potential to enhance the general welfare.

2 **Students will demonstrate an understanding of how the many dimensions of this global interrelatedness developed over time.**

The global interrelatedness we are now experiencing is not a new phenomenon; it has been growing throughout much of the history of human life on this planet. Through global education, children are introduced to a profile of human history that traces the evolution of global connections as human beings and their technologies have spread over the face of the planet. They begin to understand the significance of the migration of peoples, the development of economic systems, and advances in technology. They see how systems have always been intertwined and how these connections are increasing as the world becomes more complex.

---

3 **Students will demonstrate how global links affect their role as citizens of one nation among other nations.**

A quality education for the 21st century makes explicit the fact that the decisions and actions of human beings have shaped and continue to shape the human condition and the nature of the interdependent world in which they live. It emphasizes the fact that each "event" throughout history was the unfolding accumulation of decisions made or avoided and actions taken or not taken by people. Such examination reveals the human potential and responsibility for shaping conditions on earth in the present and the future. It provides opportunities for children to examine how decisions made and actions taken at the local and national levels affect other communities and nations. It introduces children to the various roles that citizens play at the local, national, and international levels.

---

4 **Students will demonstrate appreciation for the importance of increasing opportunities for interaction among people.**

The global links connecting people throughout the world provide increasing opportunities for people to work together to enhance the welfare of the planet and humankind. A quality education based in a global perspective gives attention to the ways that people have cooperated throughout history to address issues and solve social problems. It emphasizes the many, diverse, and distinct roles that people have played and the contributions that different individuals and groups have made in improving life on earth. Children who are prepared for the 21st

century develop cross-cultural communication skills and learn how to work with others to generate and evaluate alternative solutions to problems. They develop their ability to carry out collaborative projects with people of diverse ages, cultural heritages, and social positions. They learn how to use a full range of communication technology in working with others in their communities and across the globe.

Caring Outcomes

Each of the caring outcomes discussed in relationship to human beings, Planet Earth, and national citizenship facilitates our capacity to live full and complete lives in an interrelated world. Once again, a sense of efficacy is essential in coping with this dimension of our lives. The interrelatedness of the human condition makes it especially critical that children develop caring outcomes in relation to living on this planet.

Through an integrated global education, children CARE about:

- Developing constructive responses to diversity
- Being able to deal with change in all its manifestations
- Realizing and accepting ambiguity as part of life
- Using constructive methods to handle conflict

---

1 **Students will develop constructive responses to diversity.**

Global education is primarily concerned with two forms of diversity: diversity in human physical features and cultural patterns and diversity in access to and use of resources. Human mobility has brought the broad range of human cultural and physical diversity within the experience of most people. Visitors from abroad flow in and out of our communities. We travel, we move, the world comes to us through the media. Our children attend school with others whose heritage and experiences are very different from their own. Children in today's classrooms will confront human diversity to a degree never before possible in history.

Resources are not equally distributed either within local communities or over the planet. Nor are all groups of people equally able to tap into and use available resources. Such inequitable distribution and use present some of the most complex moral, ethical, political, and economic challenges confronting humankind.

Developing constructive responses to diversity involves recognizing and respecting diversity in human physical features and cultural patterns. It means identifying the sources of diversity and accepting diversity as inevitable and natural. Children must recognize the moral complexity inherent in diversity and seek humane solutions for the moral and ethical dilemmas growing out of diversity.

2 Students will demonstrate the ability to deal with change in all its manifestations.

Children who care, think, choose, and act must learn to deal with the personal life changes they will experience and the rapid and extensive social changes that will characterize the 21st century. It is imperative that children be neither frightened by nor enamored of change. If frightened, they will be incapable of accepting changes over which they have no control or of monitoring changes that are potentially manageable. On the other hand, if they welcome change for its own sake, they will be oblivious to the potentially harmful consequences of some changes.

In developing constructive responses to change students must perceive change as inevitable and natural. They must be shown how to respond positively to desirable change and how to condemn or impede undesirable change. The broader meaning and ramifications of change must be explored. Children must be assisted in recognizing and responding humanely to the moral complexities of change.

3 Students will accept ambiguity as part of life.

What we "know" depends on our past experiences, our intelligence, our perspectives, and our access to information. Each of these is limited and usually changing, yet we must act. An integrated global education helps children develop constructive responses toward ambiguity by helping them to perceive ambiguity as inevitable and natural and giving them the competence and courage to act effectively in the face of uncertainty. Young people need to be shown how to acknowledge when information is lacking and how to find answers. They can be provided resource and reference materials that offer different accounts, interpretations, and data about a given event. They can be taught to evaluate the strengths and weaknesses of mass media, responses to questions, and data they collect through direct observation. They can be encouraged to discuss political and social issues. The study of history can give students insight into the shifts in human knowledge and in our assumptions of what is true.

Effective integrated global education prompts children to seek alternatives; to be open–minded; to accept and even encourage conflicting interpretations of events, poems, news articles, and scientific data; to refuse to be intimidated by not knowing an answer; and to be willing to search for answers.

4 Students will use constructive methods to handle conflict.

A world that is diverse, changing, and ambiguous is also full of conflict. Children who learn to manage conflict effectively in their everyday social lives will be able to transfer those skills to managing conflict on the national and international level. Conflict is inevitable and natural because human beings are separate, individual persons with unique wants and needs who live in the company of others. Conflict, of course, can and does occur at any level of human interaction. Parents and teachers are all too aware of the interpersonal conflict among young human beings because it so often is expressed very openly. At the other end of the continuum is conflict on a global scale.

Developing constructive responses to conflict involves recognizing conflict as inevitable and natural and not being traumatized by conflict. It means having confidence in one's own capacity to work through a contentious situation. Students must perceive conflict as potentially manageable and must learn to use alternative methods of conflict management. Becoming adept at recognizing and responding to the moral complexities inherent in any conflict situation is a primary goal of global education.

Thinking Outcomes

The development of higher order thinking skills is important in each of the messages of this framework, but it becomes even more important when discussing and exploring the meaning of living in an interrelated world. Paramount in a global education is the development of the thinking skills required to deal with the complexities of interdependent systems and the natural friction resulting from this interdependence.

Through an integrated global education, children THINK about:

- Evaluating actions and inaction, both collective and individual
- How actions can lead to consequences that can enhance or endanger life in other countries and on this planet
- Comparing and contrasting entities to better understand relationships

1 Students will evaluate collective and individual actions and inaction.

This evaluation process calls for children to make judgments about such things as the goodness or

badness, accuracy or inaccuracy, and desirability or undesirability of selected phenomena. The process also calls for children to solve problems, seek answers to complex questions, or select appropriate courses of action when given selected criteria. Children become competent evaluators by generating multiple alternatives when exploring a question or solving a problem and by learning to make rational judgments based on well-founded values. Recognizing that actions affect people differently and factoring such human consequences in when making judgments are signs of evaluating actions. Children who make evaluations in an explicit and reflective manner are learning the thinking skills needed in an interrelated world.

2 Students will demonstrate an understanding of how actions can lead to consequences that can enhance or endanger life in other countries and on this planet.

In a world of interrelated systems, the major tenet that should guide all actions is the knowledge that actions have consequences; that is, any change causes other changes. This problem-solving approach recognizes and capitalizes on the fact that people are key to identifying and solving any problem. It recognizes that the differing perspectives and values that people hold must be considered in approaching any problem. A systemic approach to problem solving works against quick fixes that appear to correct a problem but actually create or exacerbate other problems.

3 Students will compare and contrast entities to better understand relationships.

When two or more things are compared, they are examined for both their similarities and differences. Thus, comparing involves what are commonly identified as two skills, comparing and contrasting. Comparing and contrasting involves looking at similarities and differences cross-sectionally and longitudinally. Children are developing competency in comparing and contrasting when they are able to make increasingly complex comparisons of the attributes, qualities, or properties of two or more different entities (e.g., two children, an American family and a Vietnamese family). Another sign of growing competency is the ability to compare and contrast the same entity at different points in time (e.g., an individual in infancy, childhood, and old age; U.S. technology in the 19th and 20th centuries).

Choosing Outcomes

Making choices is always difficult and becomes more so when using a global perspective, for then we must often keep in mind not only the effects on the individual and immediate community, but also the effects on other people in communities far away. It is imperative that we be open to new information, willing to modify our choices, and prepared to work with others to reach the best possible decisions.

Through an integrated global education, children CHOOSE to:

- Keep an open mind and a willingness to change actions and opinions when new information or evidence comes along
- Continue working on a problem or research project until the best possible solutions or answers are uncovered
- Work with others to solve problems and develop mutual understanding

1 Students will demonstrate a willingness to be open to new information and to alter their opinions based on new information.

Living in an interrelated, constantly changing world is a challenge requiring a willingness to be open to new and ever changing information. Decisions must be made, but a global education will teach children the need to alter direction when new information

dictates. Making decisions in this way requires the ability to keep an open mind and the confidence to change opinions based on up-to-date data.

2 Students will demonstrate persistence in seeking the best possible solutions.

A global education will foster in students the ability to persist in seeking solutions to difficult problems. Given the complexity and interconnectedness of the issues confronting the peoples of the world, persistence is a quality all children should have. Tenacity in the problem-solving process will result in more thoughtful solutions that reflect an appreciation for and understanding of the messages of this framework.

3 Students will work with others to solve interrelated problems.

Children develop skills of collaboration and cooperation when they work in groups to apply knowledge and to practice the skills and caring capacities identified in this framework. Cooperative activities demonstrate to students the benefits of working with others and help them develop the skills needed to solve the many interrelated problems of our planet. Teachers who systematically and routinely structure cooperative learning opportunities are enhancing children's understanding of and ability to thrive in an interdependent world. A global education will encourage students to choose joint problem solving as an effective method of dealing with personal and social issues.

Acting Outcomes

A global education provides students with an understanding of systems theory that governs their actions. With a systems orientation, students learn to base their actions on information from several sources: research, stakeholders, and their own experience. All sources of information should be considered when taking actions that will inevitably have ramifications throughout the system. A systems perspective also makes clear to students the need to collaborate with others in taking actions that address the issues of our interrelated world.

Through an integrated global education, children ACT:

- With the understanding that the world is a series of interdependent systems
- With the knowledge that human choice in determining the future is based on possibility, probability, and preferability

1 Students will demonstrate an understanding that the world is a series of interdependent systems.

People who live in an interdependent world must recognize the systemic nature of problems; they must not get mired in the negative aspects of each problem but instead see the possibilities inherent in any problem situation. Understanding the world from a systems viewpoint encourages children to embrace problems as challenges that they, together with others, can meet successfully. Through practice in solving increasingly complex and challenging problems, children hone their competencies and increase their confidence in addressing globe-spanning challenges.

2 Students will demonstrate an understanding that human choice in determining the future is based on possibility, probability, and preferability.

A global education instills in students an acceptance of life's ever changing conditions. This acceptance leads to an understanding that choices must constantly be made and that the results of those choices are governed by the possibility and the probability of success. Actions taken at a given point in time may need to be adjusted when possibilities and probabilities change. Students become comfortable with the reality that a multitude of actions are possible and, therefore, one of the criteria in deciding which actions to pursue rests with the perceived preferability of the result. Both the power inherent in human choice and the shifting circumstances in which this power is exercised are profound challenges for students acting in an interrelated world.

Part Two

SAMPLE
INTEGRATED UNITS

Walls

HELEN HERR ELEMENTARY SCHOOL
CLARK COUNTY SCHOOL DISTRICT
LAS VEGAS, NEVADA

LINDA FLEMING

BILL GILLULY

CATHY KAPPEL

JANET KING

ROD KISSINGER

KAREN MCVEIGH

Framework for Integrating Instruction Planning Form

1. Selection of Concept: Cultures

2. Formation of Key Unit Generalizations:
- Walls serve as a reflection of the culture of people.
- Walls are both positive and negative in nature.
- Walls are used for a variety of purposes.
- Walls come in a variety of forms.

3. Key Questions:
- What is a wall?
- How are walls used by cultures?
- Are walls good or bad?
- How can walls reflect a culture's history?

4. Formation of Activity/Content Generalizations:

Language Arts	Social Studies	Science	Math	Other
Walls convey information: stock exchange, graffiti, town walls, etc. Words can be used as walls.	Landforms can be barriers: water, deserts, rain forests, etc. Landforms influence the history and culture of people.	Machines build walls. Walls are built of different kinds of material for different purposes.	Walls have many shapes—geometric concepts such as perimeter, area, etc.	Mosaic tile walls are functional and illustrative of a people's culture.

5. Student Outcomes:
Students will explore the different forms and functions of walls by comparing and contrasting different types of walls from around the world.

They will demonstrate their understanding of key unit generalizations and activity/content objectives through:

- Journal writing
- Class discussions
- Group presentations
- Construction of mosaic walls, planes, glyphs
- Research papers

Planning Web

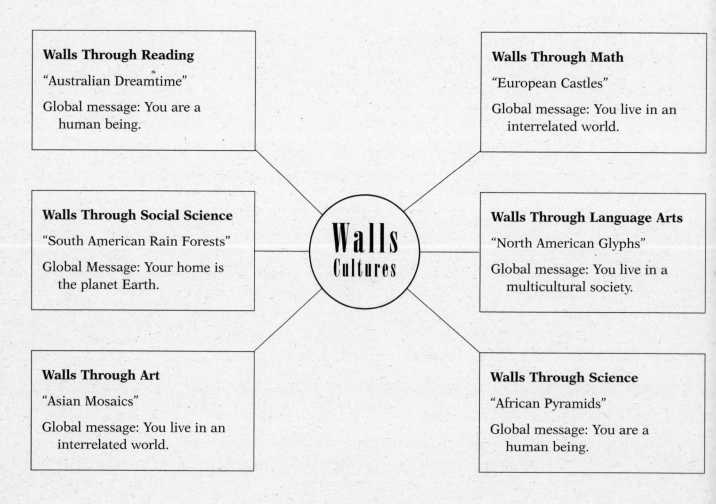

Walls Through Reading

"Australian Dreamtime"

Global message: You are a human being.

Walls Through Math

"European Castles"

Global message: You live in an interrelated world.

Walls Through Social Science

"South American Rain Forests"

Global Message: Your home is the planet Earth.

Walls
Cultures

Walls Through Language Arts

"North American Glyphs"

Global message: You live in a multicultural society.

Walls Through Art

"Asian Mosaics"

Global message: You live in an interrelated world.

Walls Through Science

"African Pyramids"

Global message: You are a human being.

ACTIVITY

Activity Title: "Australian Dreamtime"

Concept: Cultures

Organizing Topic: Continent of Australia

Theme: Walls

Discipline: Reading

Global Message: You are a human being.

Objectives:

- Read and demonstrate comprehension of a story.
- Distinguish story character.
- Give personal reaction to a story.
- Identify the author's purpose.
- Respond to different types of literature in a variety of ways.
- Recall sequence of events.
- Participate in various forms of oral communication.

Materials:

- Picture file of: Australian rock art, Native American petroglyphs, graffiti, stock exchange, and town walls
- Collection of seven or eight Australian Dreamtime stories

Procedures:

1. Show and discuss with the whole class pictures of people reading a variety of walls (stock exchange, graffiti, town walls, Native American petroglyphs, and Australian Rock Art).

2. Show various pictures of Dreamtime art from Australia.
   - Have students predict possible reasons for telling the Dreamtime stories represented by the art.
   - Have students predict what the stories are about.
   - Provide students with background information regarding the Dreamtime stories and their oral tradition.

3. Tell a Dreamtime story to the class following this format:
   - Talk about the main characters.
   - Talk about the setting.
   - Summarize the story.
   - Tell the story.
   - Give personal reaction to the story.

4. Divide the class into five or six heterogeneous small groups and provide each group with a written copy of a Dreamtime story. Each is to follow the steps modeled by the teacher in Step 3 above and do a choral retelling of the story. Groups must first decide on characters, setting, story plot, and the group's reaction to the story. Then they are to practice their story before presenting it to the whole class.

5. Group presentations

6. Lead the class in a discussion on the group presentations, comparing the choral retelling to other forms of communication used today.

Assessment:

Evaluation will consist of scores given for the oral presentation. A scoring rubric for the five steps of the presentation will be devised.

ACTIVITY

Activity Title: European Castles

Concept: Cultures

Organizing Topic: Continent of Europe

Theme: Walls

Discipline: Mathematics

Global Message: You live in an interrelated world.

Objectives:

- Investigate combining geometric figures/shapes.
- Recognize, develop patterns.
- Investigate properties of addition using objects.
- Apply strategies to solve problems within mathematical strands.
- Compare and contrast patterns, styles, purposes of walls.
- Investigate perimeter and area.
- Investigate (standard and nonstandard) measurement.

Materials:

- Photographs of walls around Europe (Castle, Berlin Wall, etc.)
- Centimeter graph paper
- Manipulatives to construct walls (color tiles, Base Ten Blocks, unifix cubes)

Procedures:

1. With the whole group, discuss reasons why people build walls; write ideas on the board. Have students discuss how walls are similar and/or different from one another in looks and purpose and what would be needed in a wall built to protect the land.

2. Show pictures of important walls from around the world (walls surrounding European castles, the Berlin Wall). Discuss the significance of the walls, change over time, similar walls in the United States, and the need for these similar walls today in our country.

3. Introduce the whole group to the *cubit*, an ancient measure based on the length of the arm from the elbow to the tip of the middle finger. Tell students the word cubit comes from the Latin word for elbow. Discuss with the class any problems they might find with using their own arm to measure things.

4. Divide the class into small groups and ask each group to design a wall containing a continuous pattern that's either purposeful or decorative. To help organize their ideas, students may use manipulatives to build a three-dimensional wall or they may draw the wall.

5. After students have developed their walls, they should transfer the wall onto centimeter graph paper. Tell students that each square represents one cubit and that they are to show at least one repeat of the wall's pattern in their drawing on the graph paper.

6. Each group will be responsible for making an information sheet about their wall, describing the pattern they created along with measurements of height, perimeter, and area of the wall, how many cubits it would take to build a wall 100 cubits long, and so on. Students should use estimation skills before calculating on the graph paper.

Assessment:

1. The teacher observes students as they work in small groups, focusing on their understanding of the concepts of area and perimeter.

2. The teacher examines each student's recording sheet.

ACTIVITY

Activity Title: South American Rain Forest

Concept: Cultures

Theme: Walls

Discipline: Social Studies

Global Message: Your home is the planet Earth.

Objectives:

- Identify locations of rain forests around the world.
- Describe the layers of the rain forest.
- Investigate the interdependent nature of the rain forest.
- Work in cooperative groups to establish student understandings.

Materials:

- Rain forest labels and animal cards
- Stories
- Tape
- Chairs
- Yardstick

Procedures:

1. Before class, mark off a 6′ x 6′ square on the floor with masking tape. This square will represent the rain forest. Create rain forest layer/animal cards, being sure to have one card for each student. You'll need a few canopy cards, several floor and emergent layer cards, and many understory cards, for the underlayer has the greatest number of life-forms.

2. Have students gather around the square and briefly describe the activity. Discuss with students how a rain forest may act as a natural wall (what are the different functions of walls?).

3. Distribute one layer/animal card to each student and have students fasten the cards to their bodies with masking tape.

4. Ask students who have the forest floor cards to come to the taped-off area and position themselves to resemble a forest floor. Describe—or have a student describe—the purpose and function of this layer. Follow this same procedure for the other layers of the rain forest.

5. Help students process the activity by asking the following questions:

    a. What did it feel like to be part of the rain forest?

    b. Do you think you got enough air and light?

    c. Did you like being who you were in the rain forest?

    d. What did you learn about rain forests?

    e. How would removing a layer of the rain forest affect another layer? (Stress the interdependence of the layers.)

6. Have students record their understandings and feelings about the experience in their journals.

Assessment:

Evaluation will be based on students' written responses in their journals and their participation in the activity.

ACTIVITY

Activity Title: Asian Mosaics

Concept: Cultures

Organizing Topic: Continent of Asia

Theme: Walls

Discipline: Art

Global Message: You live in an interrelated world.

Objectives:

- Compare and contrast mosaic tile art from Asia and other cultures.
- Analyze the visual similarities and differences in form and content by examining Islamic and Ancient Roman mosaic walls.

Materials:

- Photographs of Islamic mosaic art and mosaic walls
- Colored construction paper
- Pencils
- Rulers
- Glue
- Scissors

Procedures:

1. Show students photos of Islamic mosaic art and mosaic walls from the ancient Roman capital of Ravenna on the Adriatic coast (402 A.D.). Ask students to speculate on the choice of materials used and their manufacture.

2. Ask students to scan the examples for similarities in subject matter, color, and composition.

3. Ask students to look for obvious differences in technique, subject matter, and patterns and to offer reasons for their answers.

4. Place students in groups of five to produce a paper mosaic "wall" using one of the following guidelines:

   - Use a theme chosen from the examples.
   - Use colors seen in the examples.
   - Use a technique shown in the examples—e.g., torn paper shapes that fit empty spaces, as in Ravenna, or carefully cut geometrics, as in Islamic designs.

Assessment:

Students will be evaluated on how well they understand mosaic tile wall art, as evidenced by their choice of mural topic, the form and composition of the images they use, the visual content of their finished product, and their group responses to aesthetic scanning of the Apse Dome of Mosaics of San Apollinare (549 A.D.) in class. Scanning will include an identification of subject matter, the achievement of balance and symmetry in the work, speculation on the use and placement of symbols and individual elements of the work. Other evaluation criteria will include the ability to work in groups, craftsmanship, and participation in class discussions.

ACTIVITY

Activity Title: African Pyramids

Concept: Cultures

Organizing Topic: Continent of Africa

Theme: Walls

Discipline: Science

Global Message: You are a human being.

Objectives:

- Learn about some simple machines to gain an understanding of how the Egyptian pyramids were built.
- Construct an inclined plane.
- Formulate and test a hypothesis.
- Gather and compare data.

Materials:

- Pictures of the Egyptian pyramids
- Board (4´ to 6´ long)
- Bricks
- Paper
- Pencil
- Stack of textbooks
- Piece of string
- Spring scale

Procedure:

Part A

1. Briefly discuss how the pyramids formed a "wall" and why Egyptians built the pyramids.

2. Discuss how machines help people do work. Show several pictures of the Egyptian pyramids and speculate on the size and weight of the blocks that make up the pyramids. Encourage students to share their ideas about how the Egyptians may have lifted the blocks into place.

3. Show students a board and bricks and tell them to write a paragraph suggesting how they could use these materials to make a machine that will lift heavy objects.

4. Demonstrate how a lever works by placing the board over the bricks in a see-saw fashion. Have a student stand on one end of the board, while another pushes down on the other end until the student is lifted off the ground.

5. Discuss these vocabulary words: load, fulcrum, and force. Have students write their conclusions about how the lever was able to lift the student, and encourage them to use the vocabulary words in their explanation.

6. Conclude the lesson with a discussion about how the Egyptians used levers to lift and turn large blocks of stone.

Part B

1. Place students in cooperative groups. Each group should have a stack of textbooks, a brick, a piece of string, and a spring scale. Students will tie the brick to the spring scale, lift the brick to the top of the stack of books, and record the force needed to lift the brick.

2. Students will write a paragraph hypothesizing how they can get the bricks to the top of the stack by using less force than lifting. Allow time for students to share ideas.

3. Next, have each group prop a board against the top of the stack of books. Then students will drag the brick up the board using the spring scale, and record the amount of force needed to drag the brick to the top. Have students compare the amount of force exerted by lifting the brick and by pulling it up the inclined plane.

4. Discuss how an inclined plane probably was used by the Egyptians to build the pyramids. Show how inclined planes helped the workers set the blocks into place by dragging them around the perimeter of the pyramid rather than lifting them to the top.

Assessment:

Following each lesson, students will record in their journals how they think the Egyptians used the lever and inclined plane to help build the pyramids. They should explain in their writing how these simple machines help people to do work. As a culminating activity, students will illustrate each vocabulary word and write a paragraph explaining its meaning.

ACTIVITY

Activity Title: North American Glyphs
Concept: Cultures
Organizing Topic: Continent of North America
Theme: Walls
Discipline: Language Arts
Global Message: You live in a multicultural society.

Objectives:

- Recognize the meaning of different glyphs.
- Understand that glyphs are a form of communication.
- Compare the Mayan language with the English language and find similar ideas, phrases, or events.
- Create a wall of information to communicate a particular idea using glyphs students have created for English concepts, words, and sounds.
- Develop a system of glyphs for the months of the year.
- Create a working definition for the word "wall" in relationship to the Mayan culture.
- Identify some walls used by the Maya.
- Identify the possible effects of walls in the Mayan society.

Materials:

- Butcher paper
- Markers
- Poster-size examples of Maya glyphs
- Notebook-size examples of Maya glyphs
- Poster-size sample of a stela with glyphs
- Worksheet on matching Maya glyphs and English words
- Encyclopedias
- Dictionaries
- Maya glyph dictionary (individual student copies of necessary pages)
- Calendars with holidays listed
- Blank calendars
- Overhead transparencies
- Overhead projector

Procedures:

1. Introduce the concept of *language* and have students brainstorm what a language must have in order to be considered a language system. Write students' ideas on butcher paper and save them. Repeat the process with the concept of *walls*.

2. Show students examples of Maya glyphs and ask them to give ideas about what they think they represent, how they might have been used, and who might have used them. Discuss their ideas and ask how they might find out for sure. Hand out or read to them information on the Maya and their glyph language.

3. Divide the class into small groups and give each group a glyph. First, have students predict what their glyph may represent. Then have students use a Mayan language key to identify the true meaning of the glyph. Students should try to determine why that symbol represents that particular concept, word, or letter. Have students share their ideas with the whole class.

   Next, show students a whole section of glyphs on a stela. Have them go back to the criteria they established for language and have them determine whether the Maya developed a language system.

4. After showing students places on which the Maya displayed their glyphs, ask students to determine if the places fit their definition of a wall. Point out that many Mayan calendar events were displayed on the walls of temples, on columns in courtyards, in ball courts, or even on the steps of the pyramids.

5. Divide the class into small groups and have groups solve a puzzle page matching Maya glyphs to English words. Discuss the similarities between the two languages. Discuss with students how the Maya developed glyphs for important events that are part of our culture as well.

6. Tell students that they will be writing their own glyphs on a wall or stela just like the Maya did. Students are to choose any subject and are to develop glyphs to write about this subject. They must also write a key for reading the glyphs so that the meaning of the stela can be clearly interpreted. Give students these guidelines:
   1. Pick a topic and discuss it.
   2. Write a small paragraph about the topic.
   3. Develop glyphs that can be used to write about this topic.
   4. Get glyphs approved by the teacher and then copy them onto the paper stela.
   5. Create a key to go with the stela to aid in interpretation.
   6. Give a presentation on the stela to the class and place the stela on a wall.

7. Talk about the importance time held for the Mayan people and how they communicated all their important events in connection with one of their three calendar systems. Have students look up the meanings of our calendar words. Then divide the class into twelve groups and have each one develop a glyph for one of the months.

8. Next, divide the class into eight groups. Have seven of them develop a glyph for a day of the week and have the other develop a system for showing the numbers used in years.

    Using the glyphs created by the small groups, have the class create a one–year calendar. Divide the class into twelve groups, assigning each group a month. Each group should:

    a. Use a blank calendar form and place all the necessary glyph symbols on it for their assigned month.

    b. Find the important holidays and events for that month and develop a glyph to represent each.

    c. Place all glyphs on the calendar.

9. Have each group present their calendar month to the class using the overhead projector and a transparency made of their part of the calendar. The class will comment on each group's calendar, noting strengths and recommending areas for change. Groups will then rework their designs. Finally, each group will transfer their part of the calendar onto a stela.

10. Discuss with the class the changes that would be needed if we displayed our calendars on "walls" (choices of calendars, how they would be purchased, and how our forms of communicating fit our society). Discuss how the "walls" used by the Maya affected their society (difficulty in creating, size, public display, and method of transporting this type of written communication).

Assessment:

Evaluation will be through the various projects, worksheets, and class discussions.

Diversity and Commonality

FEDERAL WAY SCHOOL DISTRICT
FEDERAL WAY, WASHINGTON

Diversity and Commonality
TEACHER BACKGROUND

Diversity is a major concept in social studies education. To understand humanity and our world, we must study the commonality of peoples and cultures, as well as their diversity. There are similarities and differences among individuals, groups, and institutions found throughout and within the geographic environments of the world. The Elementary Social Studies Curriculum in the Federal Way School District explores geography and culture in our world through the concepts of diversity and commonality.

Diversity accentuates differences, and commonality accentuates similarities. Both perspectives help students appreciate, respect, and understand both their own and other cultures. Beginning at the kindergarten level, our students will compare the cultures of different geographic regions or biomes of the world with their own. Under the theme of "Space and Place," students will learn the skills of geography as they study how peoples from the Arctic Eskimos to the Rain Forest Semai interact with their environment to meet their needs and perpetuate their culture. Students will see how cultures have changed over time as a result of interaction with other cultures.

Students will explore the commonalities and differences found in cultural universals such as family, arts, language, social organization, economic organization, and education. Themes such as "Individuals, Groups, and Institutions" will send students on a search for knowledge that will give some depth to their understanding of their own culture and other cultures. A major goal in social studies education is to help students develop the knowledge and skills to make informed decisions as citizens in a pluralistic, democratic society. This goal can be accomplished only if students understand that diversity is determined by cultural and environmental factors. We move from diversity to commonality through discussion of cultural universals, but exploration of the variety of ways in which different cultures approach those universals leads us again to diversity.

Diversity and Commonality
UNIT OVERVIEW

■ Theme I: Space/Place

Topics

1. Map Skills
   - Keys
   - Legends
   - Symbols
   - Atlas
   - Physical Maps
   - Globes
2. Global Locations
3. Land Forms and Bodies of Water
   - Mountains, Oceans
   - Hills, Lakes, Plains, Rivers
4. Critical Attributes of Desert

■ Theme II: Cultural Transmission

Topics

1. Within the Family
2. Within the Community/Institute
3. Language
   - Written
   - Oral
   - Other
4. Arts and Recreation

Culminating Outcome and Activity

Students will show knowledge of the diversity and commonality of cultural transmission by:

1. Drawing a picture and describing life as a member of a desert community family.

2. Making and labeling a diorama of a desert family. The diorama should include someone working, someone playing, and someone cooking.

3. Making a mural of a desert community in cooperative groups. The mural should include families, homes, workers, schools, and land.

Diversity and Commonality
PLANNING WEB

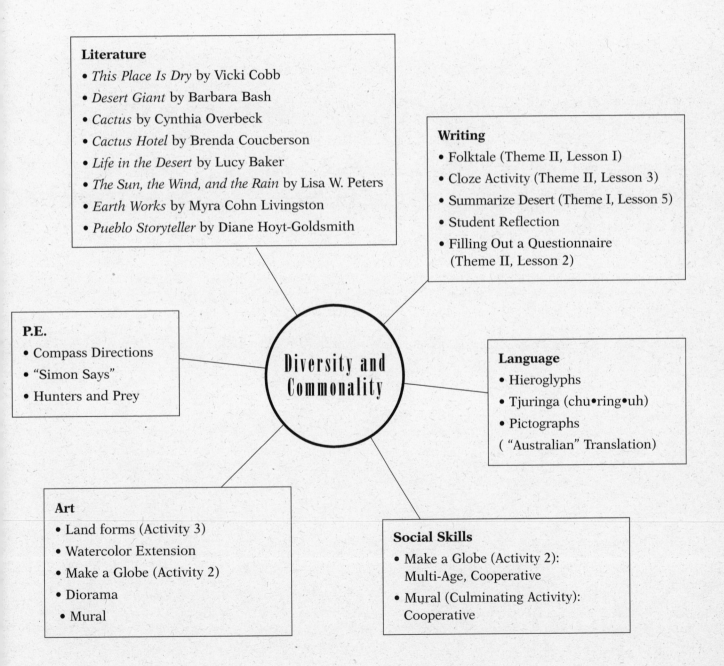

Literature
- *This Place Is Dry* by Vicki Cobb
- *Desert Giant* by Barbara Bash
- *Cactus* by Cynthia Overbeck
- *Cactus Hotel* by Brenda Coucberson
- *Life in the Desert* by Lucy Baker
- *The Sun, the Wind, and the Rain* by Lisa W. Peters
- *Earth Works* by Myra Cohn Livingston
- *Pueblo Storyteller* by Diane Hoyt-Goldsmith

Writing
- Folktale (Theme II, Lesson I)
- Cloze Activity (Theme II, Lesson 3)
- Summarize Desert (Theme I, Lesson 5)
- Student Reflection
- Filling Out a Questionnaire (Theme II, Lesson 2)

P.E.
- Compass Directions
- "Simon Says"
- Hunters and Prey

Diversity and Commonality

Language
- Hieroglyphs
- Tjuringa (chu•ring•uh)
- Pictographs ("Australian" Translation)

Art
- Land forms (Activity 3)
- Watercolor Extension
- Make a Globe (Activity 2)
- Diorama
- Mural

Social Skills
- Make a Globe (Activity 2): Multi-Age, Cooperative
- Mural (Culminating Activity): Cooperative

Diversity and Commonality
GUIDING QUESTIONS

Theme I: Space and Place

Main Point: Deserts Have a Specific Space and Place in the World

1. What are the main symbols and directions used on maps, atlases, and globes?

2a. What is a continent? Name and locate the seven continents.

2b. What is an ocean? Name and locate four oceans.

3a. How are mountains, hills, and plains different and similar?

3b. What are the similarities and differences between lakes, oceans, and rivers?

4a. What are the critical attributes of a desert?

4b. Where are the world's major deserts located?

Diversity and Commonality
THEMATIC UNIT OVERVIEW

Theme: Space and Place

LESSON	KNOWLEDGE TOPICS	GENERALIZATIONS	PROCESS SKILLS	ATTITUDES DEVELOPED
1. Map Skills	Identify continents, oceans, directions on a compass, map and globe symbols, land forms, bodies of water, location of desert regions, and critical attributes of a desert.	People use geographical reference materials to better understand their physical place in the world relative to other locations.	– Accessing reference materials – Acquiring geography map reading and research skills – Increased competence in the use of geographical reference tools 1. Locate and mark the continents, oceans, and Seattle on a map.	– Increased ability to use geographical reference tools increases self–esteem – Feeling that maps, globes ,and atlases are helpful reference materials – Increased awareness of desert regions
2. Global Location	Identify, place, and label continents.	There are seven major land areas in the world called continents. Populations live on continents.	2. Create a globe by pasting paper continents onto a blue balloon and labeling major elements.	Appreciate the diversity in size, shape, and population of the seven continents
3. Land forms and bodies of water	Identify, create, and label various land forms and bodies of water.	People use geographical terms to understand place in relation to others.	3. Create and label a collage showing mountains, hills, plains, rivers, lakes, oceans.	Recognize and appreciate the earth's variety of land forms and bodies of water
4. Orienteering	Use the compass to follow directions.	People use directional terms and instruments to better understand their place in space.	4. Orient oneself using a compass.	Develop assurance with directional terms and tools
5. Desert regions	Sort and cluster vocabulary that pertains to the desert environment. Identify desert regions.	Deserts have specific traits and are located throughout the world.	5. Use the concept attainment strategy to discover the critical attributes of a desert.	Find value in the specific traits of deserts

Unit Outcome and Activity

Students will create their own maps using modeling clay or crayons and paper. Each map should include the following correctly labeled features: mountain, hill, plain, ocean, desert, river, lake, continent, key, and compass rose. (To evaluate students' work, use the Assessment form for the Mapping Activity.)

Diversity and Commonality
THEMATIC UNIT OVERVIEW

Theme: Space and Place

ACTIVITY	PAGE NO.	REFERENCE TO GENERALIZATIONS	RESOURCES	LESSON LENGTH
1. Map Skills		Maps, atlases, and globes are useful reference tools.	• Maps • Pens • 2 blank overhead transparencies • Cards	30–40 min.
2. Global Locations		Global locations have names to help organize our world	• Globes, Continent, and Legend Blackline Masters • 100 large blue balloons • String (not in kit) • Crayons (not in kit) • Scissors (not in kit) • Glue (not in kit)	40–60 min.
3. Land forms and bodies of water		There are differences and similarities between land forms and bodies of water.	• Construction paper (not in kit) • Books • Earth songs ("The Sun, the Wind, and the Rain") • Large pictures of mountains, hills, plains, oceans, lakes, and rivers.	30–45 min.
4. Global Locations—reading a compass		There are many ways to orient yourself in the world.	• Labels • Directions for shadow tip methods • Compasses • Blank overhead • Instructions for using Direction Cards • Recording sheets	45 min.
5. Attributes of a desert		There are a variety of characteristics typical of a desert.	• Word cards (Velcro-backed) *Life in the Deserts* by Lucy Baker • Velcro chart with 2 columns: "Fits" and "Doesn't Fit" • Overhead of blackline world map • Blackline world map ditto	20–30 min.

Diversity and Commonality
LESSON OVERVIEW

LESSON NO. 1
LESSON LENGTH: 30–40 min.
GRADE LEVEL: 2nd Grade

CONCEPT: Diversity and Commonality
THEMATIC UNIT: Space and Place
TOPIC: Map skills
PAGE NO.: _____

GENERALIZATION: Maps, atlases, and globes are useful reference tools that provide visual representation of geographical environments.

Kit Materials	Lesson Extension Materials
	(Not available in Kit)
• 15 Rand-McNally laminated simplified world desk maps	
• 30 black Vis A Vis Pens	• 1 Globe
• 1 overhead transparency of a political world map including a legend, compass rose	• 1 Road Map
	• Film: *Map for Mr. Meep* VHS 17 min., 42645 (ESD#)
• Cards:	• Film: *Where Am I?* VHS 11 min., 30340 (ESD#)
– Blue tagboard cards naming oceans	
– Tan tagboard cards with green lettering naming seven continents	
• 1 overhead transparency to be used as an answer key for labeling oceans, continents	

Vocabulary (List words found in lesson)

map

atlas

compass rose

directions

continent

Diversity and Commonality
LESSON PROCEDURE

PROCEDURE	TROUBLESHOOTING AND HELPFUL HINTS
LESSON NO: 1 ACTIVITY NO: 1	(Add any information that will improve the teaching.)
1a. Teacher will hold up a map, a globe, an atlas, and a road map. "What are these? Let's brainstorm how they help us and what they do." 1b. Teacher will call volunteers to locate Seattle, USA, Australia, Africa, Pacific Ocean, and Atlantic Ocean on a globe. Teacher will identify all of these on an overhead transparency. 1c. Compass rose: "All maps share the same directions: North, South, East, West. These same directions are used on compasses by hikers, scouts, explorers." 1d. From kit: (On blue tag board) display the following cards: Atlantic Ocean, Pacific Ocean, Indian Ocean, Arctic Ocean. Ask, "What do these have in common?" (All are oceans. All are water.) (On tag board with green lettering) Teacher will display Australia, Africa, North America, South America, Europe, Asia, and Antarctica. Ask, "What do these have in common?" (All are land.) Introduce the term *continent*. Define as "one of 7 large land areas on earth." 1e. Teacher will pass out Rand-McNally maps.	Teacher may wish to keep a chart showing new vocabulary introduced throughout the unit. Teacher may find it helpful to already have cooperative groups determined before the start of this lesson. *Keep these as active groups for this entire unit.*

Objectives

1a. Identify maps, globes, and atlases.

1b. Locate home on both a map and a globe.

1c. Identify ordinal points on a compass.

1d. Name and identify: 7 continents, 4 oceans, legend, the USA, compass rose, and Seattle on a map.

1e. Define legends and symbols as used on a map.

Diversity and Commonality
LESSON PROCEDURE

PROCEDURE	TROUBLESHOOTING AND HELPFUL HINTS
LESSON NO: 1 and 2 ACTIVITY NO: 1	(Add any information that will improve the teaching.)
In cooperative groups of two, students will locate the following on a world map handout, marking each with the appropriate number: 1. North America 2. Europe 3. Asia 4. Africa 5. Antarctica 6. South America 7. Australia 8. Atlantic Ocean 9. Indian Ocean 10. Pacific Ocean 11. Arctic Ocean 12. Compass Rose 13. Legend 14. USA 15. Seattle Students will correct their work by comparing it to an overhead transparency model.	

Diversity and Commonality
Assessment Form for the Mapping Activity

Students will demonstrate a knowledge of basic map features and land forms by creating a physical map of a real or imaginary place. Students can draw the model or produce it with modeling clay. The map should contain the following features (which must be correctly labeled): mountain, ocean, hill, plain, desert, river, lake, continent, key, compass rose. Students should label each of these features.

	YES	NO
Map contains mountain.	____	____
Mountain is correctly labeled.	____	____
Map contains ocean.	____	____
Ocean is correctly labeled.	____	____
Map contains hill.	____	____
Hill is correctly labeled.	____	____
Map contains plain.	____	____
Plain is correctly labeled.	____	____
Map contains desert.	____	____
Desert is correctly labeled.	____	____
Map contains river.	____	____
River is correctly labeled.	____	____
Map contains lake.	____	____
Lake is correctly labeled.	____	____
Map contains key.	____	____
Key is correctly labeled and shows at least one map symbol.	____	____
Map contains compass rose.	____	____
Compass rose is correctly labeled with cardinal directions.	____	____
Map is neat.	____	____
Map is legible.	____	____
Spelling is correct.	____	____
TOTAL	____	____

Scoring Rubric:

3 = competent (17–21 checks in YES column)

2 = competent (12–16 checks in YES column)

1 = incompetent (0–15 checks in YES column)

Diversity and Commonality
Theme II: Cultural Transmission
GUIDING QUESTIONS

1. How is culture transmitted within a family?

2. How is culture transmitted within a community and/or institution?

3. How is culture transmitted through language?

4. How is culture transmitted through the arts/recreation?

Diversity and Commonality
THEMATIC UNIT OVERVIEW

Theme: Cultural Transmission

	KNOWLEDGE TOPICS	GENERALIZATIONS	PROCESS SKILLS	ATTITUDES DEVELOPED
LESSON				
1. Transmission of culture in a family	1. Families and the transmission of culture	1. There are similarities and differences in the ways families transmit culture.	1. Analyze the differences in the ways Aborigines, Egyptians, Pueblos transmit culture.	• Appreciate the roles and responsibilities of individuals within a family unit
	2. Communities, institutions, and culture	2. Communities and institutions transmit culture.	2. Summarize the ways culture is transmitted.	• Become concerned about the negative effects of contemporary life on culture.
	3. Language and culture	3. There are similarities and differences in the ways different desert cultures use language.	3. Compare the written language.	
	4. Cultural influences on art and recreation	4. Cultures use art in diverse ways.		

Unit Outcome and Activity
Students will evaluate the commonalities and diversity among desert communities and demonstrate understanding by making a diorama and cooperative mural depicting life in a desert community.

Diversity and Commonality
Assessment Form for Diorama and Mural Activities

Theme II: Cultural Transmission

Students will work in cooperative groups to create a diorama or mural that shows their knowledge of family life. Their creation should include the following elements: a representation of people at work, people at play, people at school, people as a family, the geographical features of desert terrain. Students should also be evaluated on their cooperative learning skills, organizational skills, and artistic skills.

	YES	NO
The student participated and contributed.	___	___
The student allowed others to participate.	___	___
The student gave supportive, positive comments to others.	___	___
The student created one (or more) representations of a home.	___	___
The student created one (or more) humans at work.	___	___
The student created one (or more) humans at play.	___	___
The student created one (or more) humans at school.	___	___
The student created a family representation.	___	___
The student showed more than one feature of a desert geographical terrain.	___	___
The student organized the mural/diorama so as to use the optimal space available.	___	___
The student used varied color and line.	___	___
TOTAL	___	___

Scoring Rubric:

3 = competent (17–21 checks in YES column)

2 = competent (12–16 checks in YES column)

1 = incompetent (0–15 checks in YES column)

Diversity and Commonality
LESSON OVERVIEW

LESSON NO. 1
LESSON LENGTH: 30–40 min.
GRADE LEVEL: 2nd Grade

CONCEPT: Diversity and Commonality
THEMATIC UNIT: Cultural Transmission
TOPIC: Family
PAGE NO.: _____

GENERALIZATION: Culture is often transmitted within a family through the telling of legends.

Kit Materials	Lesson Extension Materials (Not available in Kit)
30 copies of *Life in the Deserts* by Lucy Baker (Scholastic Inc.) Book: *The Cactus Hotel* by Brenda Coucberson Book: *The Dragon Fly's Tale* by Rodanas	

Vocabulary (List words found in lesson)

Aborigines

Legends

Diversity and Commonality
LESSON PROCEDURE

PROCEDURE	TROUBLESHOOTING AND HELPFUL HINTS
LESSON NO: 1 ACTIVITY NO: 1	(Add any information that will improve the teaching.)

Teacher: "Today we will begin to discover a group of desert-living people from Australia. These people are commonly called Aborigines.
 	
• Find Australia on globe (this will be a review of the Theme I continents lesson)
 	
• Instruct students to turn to the story "The Goomble-Gubbon" at the end of *Life in the Desert.*
 	
• In many cultures, stories are told and retold by parents to children. These stories are called *legends*. Legends are used to tell why or how something happened or came to be.
 	
• As we read this story:
 	
  1. What is the storyteller trying to explain?
 	
  2. Think of a story you know that is similar.
 	
  3. Give some characteristics of the Goomble-Gubbon.
 	
  4. What makes a desert?	

Diversity and Commonality
LESSON PROCEDURE

PROCEDURE	TROUBLESHOOTING AND HELPFUL HINTS
LESSON NO: 1 ACTIVITY NO: 1 and 2	(Add any information that will improve the teaching.)
Explain that: The rules of a group, the way people work, play, and live is called *culture*. Culture is shared by all members of a group. Culture is passed from one member to another. **Activity:** Have children draw their favorite part of the story and write one or two sentences to summarize it.	

Diversity and Commonality
LESSON PROCEDURE

PROCEDURE	TROUBLESHOOTING AND HELPFUL HINTS
LESSON NO: 1, Day 2 ACTIVITY NO: 2	(Add any information that will improve the teaching.)

• "Remember the story we read about Aborigine legends? Today we are going to continue this activity, but we are going to look at the legends of another desert society. Today we are going to discuss a legend of Pueblo Indians."
 	
 • Review:
 	
   1. What is a legend?
 	
   2. Why might a culture have use for legends?
 	
   3. Find the southwest United States on a map.
 	
 • Read Story: *The Dragon Fly's Tale* by Rodanas
 	
 • Discuss critical elements of survival in the desert.
 	
 • Activity: Use pipe cleaners to construct a dragon fly.	

Diversity and Commonality
LESSON PROCEDURE

PROCEDURE	TROUBLESHOOTING AND HELPFUL HINTS
LESSON NO: 1, Day 3 ACTIVITY NO: 3	(Add any information that will improve the teaching.)
• Remind children what a legend is. • Explain that today's legend is from a desert group called the Egyptians. • Show Egypt on a map. • Read Story: "Theresa's Looking" • Discuss the story.	

Diversity and Commonality
LESSON PROCEDURE

PROCEDURE	TROUBLESHOOTING AND HELPFUL HINTS
LESSON NO: 1, Day 4 ACTIVITY NO: 4	(Add any information that will improve the teaching.)
• To generalize the various aspects of the desert: Read *Cactus Hotel* by Barbara Coucberson Read *Desert Giant* by Barbara Bush • Prewriting activity: Have students brainstorm to come up with the names of animals that live in the desert and to describe what else they'll see in the desert. You might also give them a story-starting sentence. • Writing activity: Write your own legend explaining how deserts might have come to be. Be sure to include some possible animals that live in the desert. Tell how your desert looks and smells, and include some land forms.	Students may do this project individually or in small groups.

Diversity and Commonality
Theme II: Cultural Transmission
SUMMARY OF ACTIVITIES
FOR ASSESSING STUDENT LEARNING

1. Each student will draw a picture and describe his or her life as a member of a desert community.

2. Each student will make and label a diorama of a desert family that includes someone working, someone playing, someone cooking, land forms, and animal life.

3. Working in cooperative groups, students will make a mural of a desert community. The mural should include families, homes, workers, schools, and land.

4. Students will reflect on the quality and content of their work, either orally or in short written anecdotes. Here are some examples of questions you can use to spur thinking: What did you enjoy doing best? What was most difficult for you? What would you do differently next time? How can you improve your efforts? How well did you work in a group?

Part Three

PERFORMANCE ASSESSMENT
IN GLOBAL EDUCATION

Introduction

Assessment is the cornerstone of a sound program that incorporates global perspectives and draws upon interdisciplinary concepts and ideas. A global education is one that encourages students to gather and use information in ways that help them become productive citizens and caring human beings. It uses large themes and big ideas as organizers for studying specific content and expects students to grapple thoughtfully with complex issues. Many of the traditional assessment tools are inadequate for giving teachers, parents, and the children themselves the information they need to make sound judgments about the effectiveness of these programs and to make program decisions that continually improve the teaching/learning process.

The goals for a global education program, established by local communities, must be measured against authentic demonstrations of knowledge and action. The choice of appropriate teaching/learning activities should be informed by answers to two questions: *Why am I doing this?* and *What do I expect to happen as a result of this activity?* Assessment practices should identify what the students have taken from the activity and what has been important and meaningful to them. They should help document students' evolving understanding of concepts over time. Assessment information should help both teachers and students to understand the processes students used to achieve understanding and should lead to the identification of improved strategies for learning and doing.

Tools such as multiple-choice tests may provide some useful assessment information, but they must be matched to the curriculum at the classroom level and coupled with other devices to provide a more complete view of the knowledge, skills, and habits the students are acquiring. As Roger Farr (1994) of Indiana University explains, a multiple-choice test will tell you if a student can name different kinds of hammers, but it cannot tell you if that student can hammer a nail into the wall or if she can build something that will last.

Recommendations for performance-based assessment have been discussed since the days of John Dewey, but in recent years, educational reform efforts have led to increased experimentation with this form of assessment. Although we still have much to learn about performance-based assessment, particularly in establishing reliability and validity, we must remember that good assessment mirrors good teaching and, at least on a classroom scale, there are many good examples of ways to organize assessment that extend and expand access to information for improved teacher and student decision making.

Some basic definitions may be helpful in planning assessment strategies. *Performance assessment* is generally used to describe all forms of alternative assessments that require students to demonstrate knowledge and skill in authentic ways that reflect real-life situations and do not rely on standardized multiple-choice questions. *Performance assessment* has been defined by Marzano, Pickering, and McTighe (1993) as

> [a] variety of tasks and situations in which students are given opportunities to demonstrate their understanding and to thoughtfully apply knowledge, skills, and habits of mind in a variety of contexts. These assessments often occur over time and result in a tangible product or observable performance. They encourage self-evaluation and revision, require judgment to score, reveal degrees of proficiency based on established criteria, and make public the scoring criteria. They sometimes involve students working with others.

Performance assessments assume many different forms. All require that students *do* something that allows both the young person and the teacher to assess the student's learning, using established criteria that are clear to both student and teacher.

Constructing or identifying performance assessment tools is in many ways identical to building or selecting a good teaching device. It requires knowledge of one's students; an understanding of effective teaching/learning processes, cognitive theory, and specific academic content; and experience with assessment methodology. Baker and colleagues (1993) suggest that in evaluating assessment devices one should consider both design criteria (cognitive complexity, linguistic appropriateness, content quality, content coverage, and meaningfulness) and effects criteria (transfer and generalizability, instructional sensitivity, fairness, systemic consequences, and practicality and costs).

Creating a rubric or set of criteria for assessing performance-related tasks is still a new process for many educators. Perhaps the most knowledge exists about the development of rubrics for assessing student writing. Educators have less experience with establishing criteria for exhibitions and portfolios. Yet the process for establishing criteria remains much the same for all performance-based tasks. It is important to have a clear idea of what achievement of a learning goal looks like *in practice* and to be able to describe with clarity different levels of progress toward meeting the goal. Once these performance standards have been set and clearly described, they need to be organized into rubrics, anchor papers (samples of student papers at each assessed level), or anchor tapes (video- or audiotapes to use as guides in assessing student work). Most agree that criteria should be established in direct relation to the specific performance task, but should use consistent language across different tasks to describe particular forms of knowledge or skill.

Several key issues must be considered when establishing a system of performance assessment. Particularly pertinent to schools implementing the Global Education Framework are the following:

• ***Professional Development/Training.*** In almost every discussion of performance assessment, there is a strong emphasis on teacher training and preparation. It is essential for those who will be developing assessment tools and rubrics, rating student work, or supervising the assessment process to have a strong understanding of what purpose the assessment tool serves and how to go about eliciting an appropriate response. Teachers must be acutely aware of the extraneous performance requirements that a particular activity may require of a student. They must carefully consider what embedded assumptions they might have about prior experience or other pertinent activities conducted either at home or in class.

• ***Cultural Bias.*** It is important to recognize cultural bias and to determine what else the assessment may be measuring. Barbara Stanford of the Arkansas International Center at the University of Arkansas at Little Rock reminds us of the importance of this when describing a student response in an assessment activity involving student-produced dramas:

> An interesting sidelight on the African drama project. One 7th grader wrote a drama in which a family was captured as slaves, and when they arrived in America, they stole a canoe and rowed back home.
>
> An American scholar's response was 'How terrible that a seventh grade student knew so little about geography!'
>
> An African scholar's response was 'How wonderful! That child really understood the depth of Africans' love of freedom, how many thousands of people fled slavery even when there was no chance that they would survive' (Stanford 1994).

• ***Integration, Aggregation, Accountability.*** Performance assessment tools should be used alongside a wide array of tools for assessing learning. Within the context of each school community, there should be much preliminary discussion and agreement about what the prevailing goal of assessment is and about what those in the school community believe it should be. A very important step in this process is to inform and educate the public as to the ramifications of the many, diverse forms of assessment, emphasizing the validity and utility of alternative methods of measuring accomplishment.

To use performance assessments exclusively to evaluate classroom teaching and learning and then to exclusively use standardized tests for district and/or state accountability (as well as student certification, program evaluation, etc.) could prove detrimental. If the move toward performance assessment is not congruent with the needs for accountability, there may be little coherence and/or consistency to the assessment process with resulting confusion, particularly for parents and community members.

Many questions remain as to whether performance assessments, particularly portfolios, are adequately generalizable. Many proponents have reservations about the standardization of portfolios, which, they say, could possibly change the very

nature of portfolio assessment. Many argue that the structure and limitations that might be forced upon portfolios in order to use them as large-scale assessments would inherently obstruct the purpose and the flexible nature of the portfolio. There are particular concerns for how language-minority students may fare, should the movement toward standardization of portfolios succeed, even across a single school and especially in light of potential cultural biases mentioned above.

In the chapters that follow, we will describe in some detail three types of performance assessment devices matched to the Global Framework presented in this book. We will discuss the ways in which you can establish your own criteria for assessing student performance using these and similar assessment tools. At the time of this writing there are few, if any, examples of validated assessment tools in global education. The ones we have chosen may be said to have face validity, but they have not been tested in more rigorous ways. As more and more schools begin to implement performance assessments, we must all assume responsibility for ensuring that we continue to ask rigorous questions and carefully and methodically follow the results of our implementation.

Portfolios

Although portfolios have for decades played an important role in various assessment repertoires, they are now sweeping the nation as a new, alternative assessment practice. In fact, as portfolios have become more popular, more and more teachers have found them to be an excellent instructional tool for emphasizing the skills of problem solving and critical thinking.

Propelled largely by Howard Gardner's recent research, our conceptions of intelligence have expanded to include not only the types of intelligence that Gardner calls logical-mathematical and linguistic, but also musical, spatial, bodily-kinesthetic, interpersonal, and intrapersonal intelligence (Gardner and Hatch 1990). Portfolios can be designed to capture many of these alternative forms of intellectual capacities, in ways that standardized, multiple-choice tests have not previously succeeded.

■ Why Use a Portfolio?

To properly design a program addressing your class's needs, you must first establish instructional outcomes. The Global Education Framework, much like Howard Gardner, seeks to expand the standards to which we hold our students to include various types of knowledge and abilities. Because portfolios often serve as an instrument for nurturing critical thinking and self-reflection, many of the outcomes in the Framework can be addressed through the use of portfolios.

■ What Will the Portfolio Contain?

Portfolios allow teachers, as well as students themselves, to get to know their students as readers, writers, thinkers, and human beings (Reif 1990). Because of their wide use as an informal instructional tool, portfolios can vary greatly in shape and size. A list developed by Margaret Hill, Social Studies Coordinator of the San Bernardino County Office of Education in Riverside, California, suggests the following ideas for a portfolio in a history/social science class:

1. Writing sample of:
   a. position on a relevant controversial issue
   b. report of information
   c. autobiographical incident
   d. evaluation
   e. observation
   f. cause and effect

2. Creative writing on a H/SS theme
   a. poetry
   b. children's story
   c. play
   d. advertisement

3. Criticism of a film, book, or article

4. Videotape of
   a. student presentation on a topic
   b. debate or decision-making committee
   c. dramatization or simulation

5. Projects on, or investigations of, significant issues, or photographs of student work too big to put in a portfolio, with accompanying step-by-step process and explanation of what was learned and its meaning

6. Simulations, games, or computer programs designed by students

7. Original maps, charts, graphs, diagrams, or political cartoons demonstrating an idea or point of view

8. Documentation of student community service project

9. Original research/oral history project showing step-by-step development of resources, records of interviews, interpretation, and conclusions

10. Original research surveys and/or opinion polls on significant topics, and conclusions that might be drawn from them

11. Journals
    a. reflective writing
    b. speculation about consequences
    c. what if . . . ?
    d. double entry/dialectical journal
    e. view from a different perspective or voice

12. Recording of a song or copy of a drawing expressing a point of view on, or emotional reaction to, an event

13. Letters or drafts of legislation representing a proposed action on an issue to a political, community, or school leader

Activities such as these are extremely useful in documenting what students are learning about the community or issue they are studying. Notebooks or logs are an integral part of the portfolio process.

Regular use of these tools to reflect on what the students have learned offers the opportunity to cultivate students' self-assessment capacities and to alert the teacher to the types of activities that are most effective for each student. From these portfolio processes, students can begin their understanding of the social nature of human beings and how this sociability affects the way they live and communicate with all other human beings, which is one of the Framework's learning outcomes.

Portfolios, in fact, can assist in reaching and assessing many of the specific outcomes suggested by the Framework. For instance, portfolios can help demonstrate whether a student has achieved the ability to analyze and evaluate world issues, the ability to make inferences that are based on sound evidence, and the ability to construct meaning from knowledge and experience. Portfolios are an excellent way to help students keep track of what they are learning. Farr and Tone (1994) recommend that portfolios focus primarily on the learning process, emphasizing the idea of a working portfolio, as opposed to a show portfolio, which contains only the best and most polished examples of a student's work.

■ What Does a Portfolio Look Like?

Portfolios need not be complex. Teachers at Gibbs International Magnet School in Little Rock, Arkansas, have worked with alternative assessment for several years. They designed the assignment shown on [pages 85–86] to build a portfolio that would help students and teachers assess their progress as they completed a unit of study on West Africa. A portfolio similar to this could be used to collect assessment information for a learning outcome in the Framework, such as "Students will demonstrate an understanding of the ways that human beings make and depend upon culture."

Suggested Portfolio Contents

A portfolio is a way for you to organize and reflect on your own learning and demonstrate to others what you have learned. You will want to keep it neat and well organized and design an attractive cover.

Part I: What You Knew at the Beginning of the Unit

Include the mind map or predictions that you do at the beginning of the unit to show what you knew when you started the unit. If your teacher gives you a factual pretest, include it here.

Part II: A Daily Record of Your Learning

Each day you should record the main ideas that you learn from the unit. Your teacher may tell you how to record them, or you may choose whether to use a list, a paragraph, a drawing, or a mind map. You will also want to keep any handouts or study sheets in your portfolio.

Part III: Your Choice of Your Best Daily Assignments

You will frequently have short writing assignments during the unit. Select the best one of these for your teacher to grade. You may want to revise it, correct grammar, and rewrite or type it.

Part IV: Your Unit Project

Include both your final project and the research you did leading up to it.

Part V: What You Learned from the Unit

Include your final test or revisions of your mind map and predictions activity.

Part VI: Reflections on What You Have Learned

Describe what and how you have learned.

Source: Adapted from Arkansas International Center, copyright 1992.

Predictions

Imagine that you are planning to live in the community of _____.
What do you think it will be like? If you do not know, guess. There will be no penalty for
guessing or wrong answers on this assignment.

Imagine that you are standing in the center of the community. What do you think you will see?

1. What will the land look like? What kind of plants do you think will be growing?

2. What will people be living in? What will houses be made of?

3. What will the people look like? What will they wear?

4. What will people do for a living?

5. What will people do for fun?

6. Do you think people will be friendly? How do you expect them to treat you?

Source: Adapted from the Arkansas International Center, copyright 1992.

■ In What Way Is a Portfolio Assessed?

The successful use of portfolios rests on the thorough development and discussion, before implementation, of the criteria against which it will be assessed. Students, parents, and teachers must all clearly understand these criteria. Knowing in advance what will and should be valued helps avoid confusion and build community understanding. Every exercise should have a clear target of achievement that identifies what both the teacher and the student expect to learn from the assessment. A common and consistent vocabulary for standards and criteria should be instituted from the beginning to ensure collective understanding. Through an open discussion and decision-making process, students and their parents should be made to feel like partners in the project..

It is important to integrate student self-assessment and peer assessment into the portfolio assessment process. When evaluating portfolios, teachers should also keep in mind that students' own individual histories contribute to their performance and their learning; some flexibility and openness is necessary in the evaluation process. Questions with open-ended answers, rather than one correct answer, allow students to bring their life issues, culture, and so on, into their learning.

Exhibitions

Exhibitions in some form have been a regular part of most teachers' instructional repertoires for a very long time. In their most commonly used forms they have been called projects, experiments, research papers, or performances. These activities, which require some kind of product or performance, are sometimes designed for individual activity and sometimes designed for group activity. In each case, one or more students are asked to bring their knowledge, skill, and understanding to bear on a specific task. Exhibitions can serve as stand-alone assessments or can become part of a portfolio assessment process.

■ Why Use an Exhibition?

An exhibition, like other performance assessment tools, gives teachers and students an occasion to assess student progress toward one or more specific learning outcomes. Because the exhibition results in the student or group of students doing something—either generating a product or performing in some way—its principal value is in providing information that will help students understand what they must do to improve future products or performances. Likewise, it will allow teachers to clearly identify what the students need next in instruction. An appropriate exhibition, then, provides ample opportunity for students to demonstrate, and the teacher to observe, the level of their achievement.

■ What Does an Exhibition Contain?

An exhibition is not a random activity or performance requirement. The creation of an exhibition starts with careful thought about the learning outcomes to be demonstrated in the assessment process. Specific activities are selected based on the outcomes to be assessed. The description of the exhibition is explicit, drawing on both the language and categories that set the overall context for learning in the classroom. For example, Marzano, Pickering, and McTighe (1993) organize their performance tasks into three sections: a concise, but explicit description of the task; a list of content standards; and a list of lifelong learning standards. These standards are then linked to specific rubrics for each standard.

In a classroom using the Global Education Framework, one might organize a performance task by describing the task and then identifying one or more learning, caring, thinking, choosing, or acting outcomes to be demonstrated in this exhibition. Each of these outcomes must then also be matched with a rubric that delineates levels of performance for each outcome. These elements provide students both information about the task itself and information about the standards and criteria upon which it will be assessed.

■ What Does an Exhibition Look Like?

An exhibition may be an adaptation of a pre-existing classroom activity or one designed explicitly to assess a particular outcome. For example, the following exhibition could be used for primary grade students to assess some of the outcomes specified under the message "Your Home is PLANET EARTH":

Directions for Students

We have been studying the earth's people and cultures. Your task is to select a group of people you're familiar with and draw a picture that shows how they interact with their environment. Be sure to show some action in your picture.

When you have completed the first picture, think about the ways that things might be different if the same people interacted with their environment in a different way. Draw a second picture that shows those differences.

Be ready to present your pictures to the class and describe the different ways the people are interacting with their environment. Be ready to explain what happens as a result of those differences.

We will assess your drawings and explanations using the following standards:

Learning Outcomes:

- Students will demonstrate an understanding of human-ecosystem relationships.

- Students will demonstrate an understanding of the earth's cultural geography.

Thinking Outcomes:

- Students will demonstrate an understanding of the cause and effect of actions on the system of Planet Earth.

In What Way Is an Exhibition Assessed?

A rubric and examples, such as anchor papers or videotapes, must be developed for each outcome to be assessed. As Marzano and his colleagues (1993) remind us, "if a task is designed to assess three learning standards, the teacher produces three rubrics." It is important that these be written in advance and shared with the students. Constructing rubrics can be time-consuming, so teachers may want to draw upon resources that include already-developed rubrics for many general learning outcomes; see, for instance, *Assessing Student Outcomes* (Marzano, Pickering, and McTighe 1993). Often it is both appropriate and desirable to develop the rubrics with students. Those doing the assessing must also invest adequate time to be sure they understand the criteria and can apply them evenhandedly.

Another exhibition that could be used to assess outcomes related to the message "Your home is PLANET EARTH" was developed by the Maine Assessment Project for Grade 4 in 1990–91. This example, shown on the next five pages, includes both the directions for students and the rubrics for assessing this particular exhibition. Note that this assessment tool models the elements of good teaching practices, including the inclusion of prewriting activities.

90

The Maine Assessment Project
Social Studies, Grade 4
1990–1991

The Yanomama Indians: Endangered People
Connie Manter, John Moran, and Deborah Parker

The Scene:

You and your fourth grade friends have been chosen to visit the Yanomama Indians in South America! These people live in the Amazon rain forest region. They are in danger of losing their land and their way of life. *Newsweek* magazine wants you to live with and observe the Yanomama Indians. Then, you must prepare a report for *Newsweek* on what the Indians' problems are and how you would protect these special people.

The Tasks:

1. Looking at the picture [not included here].
   □ Look at the picture. Pretend you are going to climb into the log canoe.
   □ As you look at the scene in the picture, list words that describe what you would be touching, seeing, hearing, tasting, and smelling.
   □ Spend ten minutes on writing this list.

2. Reading the *Newsweek* story.
   □ After you have completed the list for each sense, your teacher will read the article aloud to the class.
   □ Please follow along as your teacher reads.

3. Writing the report.
   □ When you write your report, use information from your "senses" lists, the picture, the map, and the *Newsweek* story.
   □ In your own words, tell about the specific problems of the Yanomama Indians.
   □ Tell how you feel about these people and their importance in the world.
   □ Begin with a catchy title.
   □ Write your report in complete sentences.

Reminders:

- Put a checkmark in the box as you complete each of the tasks above.
- Sign your letter.

Students Are Our Future

* For more information on
Newsweek's Education Programs,
contact:
  Deborah Parker, Regional Manager,
  118 Hollister St.,
  Manchester, CT 06040.
  (800) 729–0492

The Last Days of Eden

The Yanomama Indians will have to adapt to the 10th century—or die.

Doshamosha-teri sits on a little hill near a bend in the clear black Siapa River, just north of the equator, in one of the least traveled regions of the Amazonian rain forest. Two dozen families of Yanomama Indians (149 men, women, and children) live there, in one dwelling furnished only with bark hammocks. They cultivate small plots of plantains, gourds, and bananas on the hillside. Beyond that the great wall of the rain forest rises, enclosing a dazzling bazaar of wild pigs, monkeys, and plumed birds. Most people in Doshamosha-teri ("Maggot-of-the-Gumba-Tree Place") have never heard of Venezuela, though they happen to live there. They have yet to invent the wheel. Their entire number system consists of "one," two," and "many." . . . Life consists of survival.

- Until now, the Yanomama have lived their lives in the rain forest away from the modern world.

- Now, 1 out of every 6 Yanomama has died because of malaria and other diseases brought in by gold miners from the modern world.

- Now, many are too sick, from starvation and disease, to raise crops and hunt animals.

- Now, the Yanomama need vaccinations from the modern world against mumps, measles, and polio.

- Finally, the Yanomama need the rights to their lands in order to hunt and fish. They also need the right to decide on how their land should be used. They may be the only people who know how to use the rain forest without killing it.

The Yanomama are the largest remaining group of tribal people on earth. It is amazing that they have lasted this long. *If we lose them, we lose part of ourselves. (Everyone) agrees that the Yanomama need to be saved. The question is, how?*

This is an adaptation of the article "The Last Days of Eden," *Newsweek*, December 3, 1990: p. 48. Copyright © 1990 Newsweek, Inc.: 251 West 57th Street, New York, NY 10019. All rights reserved.

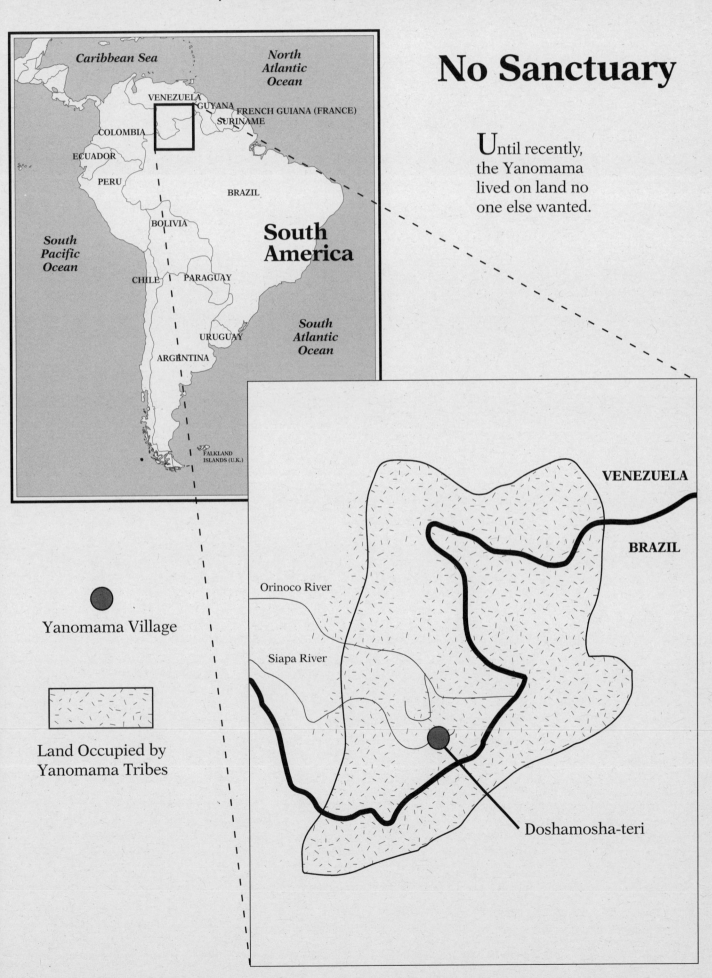

No Sanctuary

Until recently, the Yanomama lived on land no one else wanted.

Yanomama Village

Land Occupied by Yanomama Tribes

Orinoco River

Siapa River

VENEZUELA

BRAZIL

Doshamosha-teri

| The Last Days of Eden |
| Name _____ |
| School _____ |

"Senses" Lists

TOUCHING	SEEING	HEARING	TASTING	SMELLING

Report Title:

_____

_____

_____

_____

_____

_____

The Maine Assessment Project
Social Studies
1990–1991

Maine Department of Education and Newsweek Education Division

Prewriting for the Report

1. To what extent were the descriptive "senses" lists completed?
    1. no senses   2. some senses   3. all senses

2. Were the senses categorized appropriately?
    1. not at all   2. somewhat   3. fully

Writing the Report

3. To what extent were the senses listed in the columns used in the report?
    1. not used.   2. used a few times   3. used several times

In the Report, was there evidence which shows the students used information from the:

4. Maps
    1. no evidence   2. some evidence   3. considerable evidence

5. Pictures
    1. no evidence   2. some evidence   3. considerable evidence

6. The text from the *Newsweek* article
    1. no evidence   2. some evidence   3. considerable evidence

7. Did the students use their own words in the report?
    1. not at all   2. sometimes   3. throughout

8. Were the specific problems of Yanomama Indians presented?
    1. not presented   2. a few presented   3. more than two presented

9. To what extent did students express feelings about these people?
    1. none indicated   2. some attempt   3. fully present

10. Did the students express the importance of the Yanomamas in the world?
    1. no indication   2. some sense   3. fully sensed

11. Would you consider the title "catchy" and appropriate for the report?
    1. no   2. catchy but inappropriate   3. catchy and appropriate

12. To what extent were complete sentences used in the report?
    1. no complete   2. some complete   3. sentences complete

13. To what extent did the students follow the directions given in the "Tasks" section?
    1. did not follow   2. followed some   3. followed most

14. Was the report extended or enriched? (Did they go beyond the basic tasks?)
    1. no extension   2. some extension   3. definite extension

15. If you were the editor of *Newsweek Junior,* would you recommend that report be published? (Overall effect)
    1. rejected   2. use with editing   3. publish

Your Turn

16.

17.

18.

Simulations and Role Plays

Simulations and role plays have long been viewed as effective teaching devices, particularly in social studies and language arts and, more recently, in science and environmental education. Simulations allow students to participate in scenarios that imitate certain dynamics of real-life situations. Role plays allow students to dramatize situations they have studied, assume different roles and perspectives, and explore alternative endings and outcomes. Traditionally, these types of exercises have not been used as assessment devices; in fact, many people have argued that student performance in these activities should not be evaluated or formally assessed. As more people recognize the limits of traditional assessments and the importance of authentic assessment to the learning process, this argument is being reevaluated.

■ Why Use a Simulation or Role Play?

Simulations, perhaps more than any other learning and assessment activity, can demonstrate progress toward the general student outcomes of the Global Education Framework. They require that students think, care, choose, and act in a situation that approximates life. Although never able to duplicate the complexity of a real event or teach specific facts, a simulation may allow students to exercise problem-solving skills, use acquired knowledge, and experience some of the feelings that occur in a real event. Well-designed simulations may provide information that has been traditionally difficult to assess, such as the achievement of outcomes like these:

- Students will demonstrate an understanding of others' point of view through using and evaluating

appropriate skills of observation, perspective taking, reasoning, problem solving, and decision making.
- Students will ask questions that demonstrate the need to understand human beings and their actions.
- Students will seek additional information about themselves, others, and the situation before making decisions.

Role plays provide students another important avenue for demonstrating their knowledge, understanding and thinking habits. More defined in structure than simulations, they provide an excellent opportunity for students to use their abilities in dramatization and speech to demonstrate the level of attainment of certain learning outcomes. They are especially effective in allowing students to take on the role of another person and thus develop a better understanding of how that person might think and act in a given situation. A role play would be an effective assessment tool for assessing outcomes such as these:

- Students will actively obtain information about others to inform their decisions and to understand the contexts within which other people make decisions.
- Students will use their imaginations to envision alternatives that benefit all human beings.

■ What Will the Simulation or Role Play Contain?

Simulations are far more complex to develop than most learning or assessment tools. Each simulation creates an artificial situation in which students assume specific roles, according to a set of predefined rules. Although a simulation involves a form of role play, a certain degree of ambiguity is intentionally left in order to leave room for students to bring their prior experience and personal values to the activity. A simulation requires a carefully designed set of facilitator instructions for the teacher; may require certain student materials; and should include suggested questions and instructions for debriefing at the end of the activity. Participants should receive a clear, concise introduction to its framework. As rules and roles are explained, time should be allowed for questions and practice. The focus, however, should remain on the framework of the activity, and the teacher should avoid comments or answers that suggest strategies or infer outcomes.

In contrast, a role play asks students to reenact something specific they have read or studied, to create an improvisation about a specific situation, or to develop alternative endings for a particular situation. It requires little facilitation and the rules are simple. Generally, a situation is defined, roles are assigned, and the students carry out the role play.

What is new for many people is the definition of standards or outcomes for the simulations and role plays and the explicit communication of those standards to students *before* the activity.

■ What Does a Simulation Look Like?

To better understand the idea of a simulation, let's look at a simulation that could be used to assess the Acting Outcomes of the Framework's message "You are CITIZEN of _____, a multicultural society." It involves the classic activity known as Broken Squares (SPICE 1994). This simulation gives students a group task that requires cooperation for successful completion. Its simple structure and time frame make it ideal for assessing outcomes such as these:

- Students will cooperate with others for the good of all societies.
- Students will make decisions using consensus processes.
- Students will communicate with others.

Overview of the Simulation

Each group of five participants will receive pieces of broken squares. Together, these pieces form five complete squares of equal size. The pieces allotted to each individual, however, do not form one of the desired squares. The group task is to find the right combination of pieces to form five squares of equal size. At the end of the activity, each group member must have one complete square equal to the squares of the other group members. There are only three rules which group members must obey in accomplishing their joint task:

- No member may speak.
- No member may take a piece from another group member, nor in any way signal that he wants a piece.
- Members may give pieces to one another.

These rules make it clear that sharing and cooperation are necessary for the group task to be completed.

Objectives of the Simulation

Participants will:

- Explore methods of problem solving involving cooperation and/or competition.
- Experience the need for cooperation in accomplishing a mutual goal.
- Investigate characteristics of a society and how members of a society work together, using knowledge of their own society as a basis.

• Analyze the concepts of cooperation and competition, and the potential role each may play in a society and between societies.

Preparation for the Simulation

You will need:
• Heavy colored construction paper
• Five envelopes per group
• A ruler
• A pair of scissors
• A magic marker

You need one set of five broken squares for every five participants in the class. (If your class is not evenly divisible by five, the remaining participants may serve as observers.)

To make the broken squares:

1. Cut a set of five 6" x 6" squares of the same color. (Additional sets of squares my be cut from other colors, but all five squares within a set must be of the same color.)

2. Further divide the squares according to the diagrams shown on this page.

3. Label the pieces with the letters indicated in the diagrams, and label five envelopes A, B, C, D, and E. If possible, laminate the squares at this point for more durable use. Then put all pieces labeled A in the envelope marked A, B pieces in the envelope marked B, and so on.

4. Make a copy of the Participant Handout on page 00. It states the objective of the activity and the rules for each group of five participants.

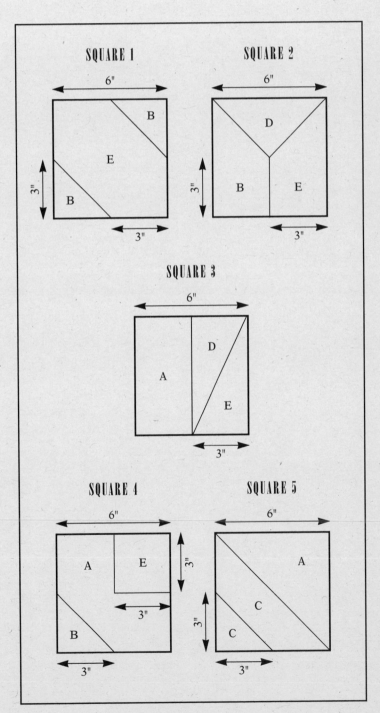

Broken Squares
Participant Handout

Objective: To form five squares of equal size, one in front of each member of the group.

Rules:

- No member of the group may speak.

- No member may take a piece from another group member or in any way signal that he or she wants a piece.

- Members may give pieces to one another.

Sharing and cooperation are necessary if the group task is to be completed!

Time

The time requirement for the simulation itself varies; however, as with any simulation, ample time for debriefing is crucial. We recommend a 45-minute session for the simulation and debriefing session. More discussion time may be allocated if you wish to address additional topics related to the experience.

Running the Simulation

1. Divide the class into groups of five. Seat each group at a table or arrange five desks in a tight circle so that group members may easily see one another's progress. In classes not divisible by five, allow remaining participants to act as observers, recording the activities of a group of their choice and monitoring the behavior of the players.

2. Explain the objective of the simulation and spell out the rules, stressing that the goal is not achieved until each group member has a perfect square and all five squares are of equal size.* You may wish to tell participants that the purpose of the exercise is to discover the best means for solving problems, or you may simply have participants play the simulation and determine the purpose afterward. Stress to participants that there is no winning or losing. Participants are simply to solve the problem confronting them—to form five equal squares from the broken squares.

*Note: Since the shapes use multiples of three inches, several combinations will form one or two equal squares, but only one combination will form five equal squares.

3. Pass out the envelopes. One set of envelopes marked A, B, C, D, and E should go to each group, and each participant in a group should receive one of the five envelopes. Instruct participants NOT TO OPEN THE ENVELOPES UNTIL THE

SIGNAL TO BEGIN IS GIVEN. Pass out a copy of the Participant Handout to each group and remind participants to refer to this sheet if they have questions during the simulation.

4. Give the signal to begin.

5. When the facilitator or participants serving as observers view behavior that is against the rules, they may choose to let the group handle it or they may intervene by reminding participants: "Members may only GIVE pieces to others," or "Remember, no talking or signaling allowed!" Such behavior will be investigated during the debriefing session.

6. When all or most groups have finished, or when participants seem to grasp the role of cooperation (versus competition) in accomplishing a mutually identified goal, call time and bring the class together for a discussion of the issues. (Note that some participants will perceive this exercise as a group task while others will interpret it as five individual tasks, with each member solely responsible for making one square. The differences between groups should be addressed in the discussion.)

Conducting a Debriefing Session After the Simulation

As with all debriefing sessions following simulations, participants must be given an immediate opportunity to describe what happened and share their feelings about the activity. Begin by asking each group to briefly describe what happened in their group. If some participants helped to monitor the activity, ask them to share their observations. Ask participants the following questions:

1. Describe what happened in your group. Did you experience problems in completing the task assigned to you? If so, how did you solve these problems? How did you feel about the activity?

2. How did you feel when someone else held a piece you or some other member of your group needed and did not see the solution as you saw it?

3. Did anyone in your group finish his square and then sit back without caring whether his solution prevented others in the group from solving the problem? How did this make you feel? What did you do about this?

4. Did anyone finish a square and then realize that you would have to break it up and give away a piece so that another person in the group could form a square? How did you come to this realization? How did this make you feel? How and why did you finally make the decision to break up your square?

5. Did you observe people in your group breaking the rules in an effort to direct the group solution? Did people take pieces from you to keep for themselves or to redistribute to others? How did you and others in your group react to such actions if they occurred? Why do you suppose the person(s) involved acted against the rules?

6. Did you feel competitive toward others in your group? Did you feel that your group was in competition with other groups? (Participant responses to these questions will vary greatly depending on the playing format the facilitator has chosen.) Did you feel compelled to finish your square before others in your group or in other groups?

7. What were your feelings toward members of your group? Did you develop a feeling of unity? If so, why? If you felt no sense of competition, what motivated you to cooperate?

8. Did you learn anything about yourself from this simulation? What sorts of things did you learn? (The facilitator may also want to relate the exercise to participants' general attitudes and relationships to each other and to the facilitator.)

Once participants have had sufficient time to describe what happened and air their feelings about the activity, have participants begin to relate the simulation to larger issues of social organization and the role cooperation plays in such organization. Ask participants to consider the foundations of society as a concept, using their knowledge of their own society as a basis for discussion. Begin the discussion with the following questions:

1. What is a society? How does the concept of cooperation fit into the notion of a society ? (Participants should emphasize various aspects of a society, such as commonality of economic, political, and/or cultural system; mutually identified goals, and so on. From their experiences in the simulation, participants should be able to ascertain that any society requires or assumes a certain amount of cooperation.

2. Can you think of a particular time in history when it was especially essential for families and groups to cooperate in joint tasks? (Participants may list such example as the early colonists, the wagon trains, quilting bees, and barn raisings.) What prompted such cooperation?

3. In what ways do you see people in our society cooperating today? (e.g., neighborhood organizations, recycling programs, charity drives, political campaigns).

4. In our society, elements of both cooperation and competition exist. What are the situations in which one predominates over the other? Why? In your opinion, is there a relationship between the notion of competition and the importance placed on individualism in our society?

5. In what instances do government officials or other leaders in our society try to persuade people to cooperate? In your opinion, are our efforts at cooperation effective? Why or why not? (Participants may choose to discuss various topics relating to cooperation, such as current attempts at energy conservation, pollution control, or crime prevention.)

When participants have explored the role of cooperation versus competition among individuals within a society, encourage them to discuss the role of cooperation and competition among various societies and nations. Have participants explore the dimensions of cooperation and competition in a global context from both a historical and a contemporary perspective. You can prompt discussion with these questions:

1. Historically, what role has competition played in the international arena?

2. Historically, what role has international cooperation played on a global scale? (Participants may mention the issue of foreign aid as an example of cooperation, as well as such international organizations as the United Nations, the World Health Organization, and UNICEF. Also, treaty alliances and various nongovernmental organizations with an international focus might be mentioned by participants as examples of cooperation on an international scale.)

3. In what forms does international competition continue to exist? Based on your experiences in the simulation, what might some of the causes for such competition be? What suggestions can you offer for resolving competitive forces that may be a potential source of international conflict?

4. What are some of the mechanisms for international cooperation in the contemporary world? Do contemporary circumstances warrant new forms of international cooperation that were not

necessary or possible in the past? (Participants may bring up such matters as advanced information and communications technology leading to increased contact among societies or global environmental concerns such as desertification or climate change.)

5. Thinking back to the suggestions made for increasing alliances from the family/clan to the nation, how can we go about enhancing people's sensitivity to their role in the international community as well as their national community?

■ How Is a Simulation or Role Play Assessed?

Assessing students' performance in a simulation or role play requires identifying specific learning outcomes in advance and developing rubrics that clearly identify different levels of achievement within those outcomes. Rather than use anchor papers, some teachers find it useful to videotape simulations and role plays, thus developing anchor tapes that identify the agreed-upon criteria in action. Others use written follow-up activities to the simulations or role plays, including logs or journals measuring the students' progress toward learning goals. In some cases, observers use score sheets linked to the evaluation criteria during the simulation itself.

Planning for Assessment

As each school plans its own implementation of the Global Education Framework, careful attention must be given to plans for assessment. As with all innovations, teachers, students, parents, and community members need to know the emerging answers to questions like these:

- Are we achieving our goals? If so, which ones, and how well?

- What is my level of mastery now? How can I improve my own performance?

- How can we improve instruction?

Assessment strategies should include an appropriate mix of assessment activities that allow students the best opportunities to demonstrate what they have learned, how they think, and how they care, choose, and act. Such a mix might include a portfolio, one or more exhibitions, a simulation, an exercise using open-ended, short-answer questions, or even commercially developed tests linked to specific textbooks or readings. The key is deciding in advance what is important to document and assess, and selecting or designing corresponding activities.

Implementing performance assessment requires the school and the community to make a genuine commitment to a serious examination of what is important to teach and to learn. It requires careful definition of learning goals and standards by students, teachers, parents, and community members. It requires identifying levels of achievement for each standard and establishing rubrics and criteria that allow for fair assessment. It requires sufficient time and resources for staff development, addressing basic assessment design and implementation issues, as well as expanding teachers' understanding of student's cognitive processes, multiple abilities and intelligences, and cultural perspectives. It requires time for pilot projects and field testing of assessment devices. Finally, it requires serious evaluation of the effectiveness and limits of each assessment tool.

Performance assessment strengthens the ability of teachers and their students to define, assess, and understand not only the products of student work, but the processes involved in creating those products. This improved understanding of student productivity provides critical information to all involved in making decisions that lead to improved learning. The benefit of having the school community not only be aware of, but effectively understand, the value and utility of performance assessment far outweighs the complexity of its implementation.

Bibliography

A Sampler of History-Social Science Assessment—Elementary. (1994). Sacramento: California Learning Assessment System (CLAS), California State Department of Education.

Arter, J.A., and R.J. Stiggins. (1992). "Performance Assessment in Education." Paper presented at the annual meeting of the American Educational Research Association.

Aschbacher, P.R. (1993). *Issues in Innovative Assessment for Classroom Practice: Barriers and Facilitators*. CSE Technical Report 359. Los Angeles: National Center for Research on Evaluation, Standards, and Student Testing (CRESST).

Baker, J., M. Carter, B. Fletcher, B. Hobgood, and R. Reagan. (1992). *My African Community*. Little Rock: University of Arkansas.

Brandt, R.S., ed. (1992). *Readings from Educational Leadership on Performance Assessment*. Alexandria, Va.: ASCD.

Burstein, L. (1989). *Conceptual Considerations in Instructionally Sensitive Assessment*. CSE Technical Report 333. Los Angeles: National Center for Research on Evaluation, Standards, and Student Testing (CRESST).

Campbell Hill, B., and C. Ruptic. (1994). *Practical Aspects of Authentic Assessment: Putting the Pieces Together*. Norwood, Mass.: Christopher-Gordon Publishers.

Cizek, G. (1991). "Innovation or Enervation? Performance Assessment in Perspective." *Phi Delta Kappan* 72, 9: 695–699.

Damico, J.S. (1992). *Performance Assessment of Language Minority Students. Focus on Evaluation and Measurement*, Vols. 1 and 2. Washington, D.C.: Proceedings of the 1991 National Research Symposium on Limited English Proficient Student Issues.

Farr, R., and B. Tone. (1994). *Portfolio and Performance Assessment: Helping Students Evaluate Their Progress as Readers and Writers*. Fort Worth, Texas: Harcourt Brace Jovanovich, College Publishers.

Gardner, H. (1990). *Multiple Intelligences Go to School: Educational Implications of the Theory of Multiple Intelligences*. Technical Report No. 4. New York: Center for Technology in Education.

Gearhart, M., J.L. Herman, E.L. Baker, and A.K. Whittaker. (1992). *Writing Portfolios at the Elementary Level: A Study of Methods for Writing Assessment*. CSE Technical Report 337. Los Angeles: National Center for Research on Evaluation, Standards, and Student Testing (CRESST).

Glaser, R., K. Raghavan, and G.P. Baxter. (1992). *Cognitive Theory as the Basis for Design of Innovative Assessment: Design Characteristics of Science Assessments*. CSE Technical Report 349. Los Angeles: National Center for Research on Evaluation, Standards, and Student Testing (CRESST).

Gordon, E.W. (1992). *Implications of Diversity in Human Characteristics for Authentic Assessment*. CSE Technical Report 341. Los Angeles: National Center for Research on Evaluation, Standards, and Student Testing (CRESST).

Herman, J.L. (1992). *Accountability and Alternative Assessment: Research and Development Issues*. CSE Technical Report 348. Los Angeles: National Center for Research on Evaluation, Standards, and Student Testing (CRESST).

Higuchi, C. (1993). *Performance-Based Assessments and What Teachers Need*. CSE Technical Report 362. Los Angeles: National Center for Research on Evaluation, Standards, and Student Testing (CRESST).

Kletzien, S.B., and M.R. Bednar. (1990). "Dynamic Assessment for At-Risk Readers." *Journal of Reading* 33, 7: 528–533.

Koretz, D., B. Stecher, and E. Deibert. (1992). *The Vermont Portfolio Assessment Program: Interim Report on Implementation and Impact, 1991–92 School Year*. CSE Technical Report 350. Los Angeles: National Center for Research on Evaluation, Standards, and Student Testing (CRESST).

Linn, R.L., E.L. Baker, and S.B. Dunbar. *Complex, Performance-Based Assessment: Expectations and Validation Criteria*. CSE Technical Report 331. Los Angeles: National Center for Research on Evaluation, Standards, and Student Testing (CRESST).

Martin-Kniep, G.O., and N. Wise. (1991). "Assessing Perspective-Taking and Related Abilities in Global Education." Paper presented at the annual meeting of the American Educational Research Association.

Marzano, R.J., D. Pickering, and J. McTighe. (1993). *Assessing Student Outcomes: Performance Assessment Using the Dimensions of Learning Model*. Alexandria, Va.: ASCD.

Newman, C., and L. Smolen. (Winter 1993). "Portfolio Assessment in Our Schools: Implementation, Advantages, and Concerns." *Mid-Western Educational Researcher* 6, 1: 28–32.

Paulson, L.F., and P.R. Paulson. (1990). "How Do Portfolios Measure Up? A Cognitive Model for Assessing Portfolios. Revised." Paper presented at the annual meeting of the Northwest Evaluation Association.

Performance Assessment Methodology. Resources in Performance Assessment. (1993). Portland, Ore.: Center for Performance Assessment, Northwest Regional Educational Laboratory.

Perrone, V., ed. (1991). *Expanding Student Assessment*. Alexandria, Va.: ASCD.

Ravitch, D. (1993). "Launching a Revolution in Standards and Assessments." *Phi Delta Kappan* 74, 10: 767–772.

Rea, D.W., and D.K. Thompson. (1990). "Designing Transformative Tests for Secondary Literature Students." *Journal of Reading* 34, 1: 6–11.

Rief, L. (1990). "Finding the Value in Evaluation: Self-Assessment in a Middle School Classroom." *Educational Researcher* 47, 6: 24–29.

Shavelson, R., G. Baxter, and J. Pine. (1992). "Performance Assessments—Political Rhetoric and Measurement Reality." *Educational Researcher* 21, 4: 22–27.

Stanford, B. (1994). Letter to Kyo Yamashiro, SPICE, Stanford University

SPICE. (1994). "Broken Squares." Stanford, Calif.: Stanford Program on International and Cross Cultural Education, Stanford University (SPICE).

Sweet, D., and J. Zimmerman, eds. (1992). *Performance Assessment*. Washington, D.C.: Office of Educational Research and Improvement.

Worthen, B. (1993). "Critical Issues That Will Determine the Future of Alternative Assessment." *Phi Delta Kappan* 74, 6: 444–454.

Resources for Global Education

Programs

Fulbright Teacher Exchange Program
600 Maryland Avenue, SW
Room 142
Washington, DC 20024
Phone: (202) 382–8586

International Education and Resource Network
(telecommunications)
The Copen Family Fund, Inc.
345 Kear Street
Yorktown Heights, NY 10598
Phone: (914) 962–5864

The Sister School Project
P.O. Box 99492
Seattle, WA 98199
Phone: (206) 286–1964 Fax: (206) 285–1543

Publishers of Material Related to Global Education

Alberta Global Education Project
11010 142nd Street, #410
Edmonton, Alberta T5N 2R1
Phone: (403) 453–2411 or (800) 232–7208
Fax: (403) 455–6481
books, institutes, curriculum materials, conferences

American Association of School Administrators
1801 North Moore Street
Arlington, VA 22209

The American Forum for Global Education
45 John Street
Suite 908
New York, NY 10038
Phone: (212) 732–8606
publications

Apex Press
c/o Council on International Affairs
777 United Nations Plaza
Suite 3C
New York, NY 10017
Phone: (212) 953–6920

Center for Global Education
University of York
Heslington, York Y0I 5DD
Teacher materials

Council for the Advancement of Citizenship
1724 Massachusetts Avenue, NW
Suite 300
Washington, DC 20036
Phone: (703) 706–3361
Resource packets on topics of citizenship education, human rights, politics, etc.

Council of Chief State School Officers
379 Hall of the States
400 North Capitol Street, NW
Washington, DC 20001–1511
Phone: (202) 393–8161
Fax: (202) 393–1228

Cultural Survival
11 Divinity Avenue
Cambridge, MA 02138
Phone: (617) 495–2562
books and quarterlies

Curriculum Association
5 Esquire Road North
Billerica, MA 01862–2589
Phone: 1–800–225–0248
books, materials, etc.

David M. Kennedy Center for International Studies
Brigham Young University
280 Herald R. Clark Building
Provo, UT 84602
publications for children and teachers

Educators for Social Responsibility
23 Garden Street
Cambridge, MA 02138
Phone: (617) 492–1764
books, videos, institutes

FLES (Foreign Languages in the Elementary School)
University of Maryland
Modern Languages and Linguistics Department
Baltimore, MD 21228
Phone: (804) 231–0824

Foreign Policy Association
729 Seventh Avenue
New York, NY 10019
Phone: (212) 764–4050
Fax: (212) 302–6123
publications for teachers and students

Global View, Inc.
2901 Connecticut Avenue, NW
Suite B–4
Washington, DC 20008
videos

National Geographic Society Educational Services
P.O. Box 98018
Washington, DC 20090
books, videos, curriculum materials

Reach Center for Multicultural and Global Education
180 Nickerson Street
Suite 212
Seattle, WA 98109
Phone: (206) 284–8584
Fax: (206) 285–2073
publications, training opportunities, newsletter, program information

Smithsonian Institution Office of Elementary and
  Secondary Education
Arts and Industries Building
Room 1163
Smithsonian Institution
Washington, DC 20560
Phone: (202) 786–2779
multicultural curriculum for early childhood

Social Studies School Service
10200 Jefferson Boulevard, Room 10
P.O. Box 802
Culver City, CA 90232–0802
books, videos, maps, etc.

South Carolina Department of Education
1429 Senate Street
Room 801
Columbia, SC 29201

SPICE
Littlefield Center, Room 14
300 Lausen Street
Stanford University
Stanford, CA 94305–5013
curriculums, units

United Nations Sales Section
Room DC2–853, Dept. 203
New York, NY 10017
Phone: (212) 963–8302
children's books, teacher materials, videos

Worldlink
P.O. Box 480483
Los Angeles, CA 90048
(213) 273–2636
videos, teachers guides, books

110

Materials for Children

Cobblestone Publishing, Inc.
30 Grove St.
Peterborough, NH 03458
Phone: (603) 924–7209
magazines and books for young people

Mershon Center
Ohio State University
199 West 10th Ave.
Columbus, OH 43201
Phone: (614) 292–1681
Peace Education Program

Perma-Bound Books
Vandalia Rd.
Jacksonville, IL 62650

Short Story International
P.O. Box 405
Great Neck, NY 11022
Phone: (516) 466–4166
books of short stories from different countries with teacher information

World Music Press
P.O. Box 2565
11 Myrtle Ave.
Danbury, CT 06813
Phone: (203) 748–1131
books, recordings, videos, choral music

Young Discovery Library
217 Main Street
Ossining, NY 10562
Phone: (914) 945–0600
Fax: (914) 945–0875
science topics for young children

Curriculum Materials

Adubon Curriculum Materials
Northeast Adubon
Education Department
Route 4
Sharon, CT 06069
classroom-ready curriculums

Center for Teaching International Relations
University of Denver
Denver, CO 80208
Phone: (303) 871–3106
classroom materials

Church World Service
P.O. Box 968
Elkhart, IN 46515–0968
videos and curriculum units

Ethnic Arts and Facts
P.O. Box 20550
Oakland, CA 94620
Phone: (510) 465–0451
curriculum

Fireworks Educational, Inc.
P.O. Box 2325
Joliet, IL 60434
Phone: (815) 725–9057
lessons and units

Global Tomorrow Coalition
1325 G Street, NW
Suite 915
Washington, DC 20005
Phone: (202) 628–4016

Goethe House New York
1014 Fifth Avenue
New York, NY 10028
Fax: (212) 439–8705

New Brunswick Global Education Center
P.O. Box 752
Frederickton, New Brunswick, E3B 5R6
Phone: (506) 452–1774
activities, readings

Population Reference Bureau
1975 Connecticut Avenue, NW
Washington, DC 20009–5728
Phone: (202) 483–1100

Social Science Education Consortium
3300 Mitchell Lane, Suite 240
Boulder, CO 80301–2272

The Teachers' Press
3731 Madison Avenue
Brookfield, IL 60513
Phone: (708) 485–5983

Wisconsin Department of Public Instruction
Drawer 179
Milwaukee, WI 53292–0179
units on American Indians

World Eagle, Inc.
64 Washburn Avenue
Wellesley, MA 02181
Phone: (800) 634–3805
teacher resource material, maps

ZPG Publications
1400–16th Street, NW
Washington, DC 20036
teaching kit

Books

American Collegiate Service
P.O. Box 442008
Houston, TX 77244
Phone: (713) 493–9863

The Center for Foreign Policy Development
Brown University
P.O. Box 1948
Providence, RI 02912
Phone: (401) 863–3465

Council on International and Public Affairs
Suite 3C
777 United Nations Plaza
New York, NY 10017
Phone: (212) 953–6920

Intercultural Press, Inc.
P.O. box 700
Yarmouth, ME 04096
Phone: (207) 846–5168
Fax: (207) 846–5181

Interdependence Press
435 North Harwood Street
Orange, CA 92666
Phone: (714) 744–2821

International Research and Studies Program
Center for International Education
U.S. Department of Education
400 Maryland Ave., SW
Washington, DC 20202

Lexington Books
866 Third Avenue
New York, NY 10022
Phone: (202) 363–7441

Massachusetts Global Education Program
Winchester Public Schools
Winchester, MA 01890

Myers-Walls
Brethern Press
Elgin, IL 60120

112

SAGE Publications, Inc.
P.O. Box 5084
Newbury Park, CA 91359
Phone: (805) 499–0721
Fax: (805) 499–0871

Toys

Global Starts Products
P.O. Box 306
Reading, MA 01867
Phone: (617) 944–1443

Global Village
2210 Wilshire Blvd.
Suite 262
Santa Monica, CA 90403
Phone: (213) 459–5188

Puzzles and Such, Inc.
P.O. Box 3118
Hutchinson, KS 67504
Phone: (306) 663–492

Telecommunications/Technology

CD–ROM, Inc.
1667 Cole Blvd.
Suite 400
Golden, CO 80401
(303) 231–9373

Educational Resources Catalog
1550 Executive Drive
Elgin, IL 60123
Phone: 1–800–624–2926
software

Global Education Motivators
Chestnut Hill College
Chestnut Hill, PA 19118–2615
Phone: (215) 248–1150
database, e–mail focus

The Global Learning Corporation
P.O. Box 201361
Arlington, TX 76006
Phone: 1–800–899–4452

IBM Systems Co.
Phone: 1–800–368–2728
CD–ROM

Tech Knowledge
128 South Ryan Street
Auburn, AL 36830

Other

AFS–International/Intercultural Programmes, Inc.
313 East 43rd Street
New York, NY 10017
Phone: (212) 949–4242
exchange program

American Society for Environment Education
P.O. Box KB
Dana Point, CA 92629
Phone: (714) 469–3238
newsletter, teacher training

Amnesty International, USA
322 8th Avenue
New York, NY 10001
Phone: (212) 807–8400
newsletter, clubs, writing campaigns

The Asia Society
725 Park Avenue
New York, NY 10021
Phone: (212) 288–6400
videos on Japan and Korea

A.W. Peller and Associates, Inc.
210 Sixth Avenue
P.O. Box 106
Hawthorne, NJ 07507–0106
materials

Baha'i International Community
866 UN Plaza
New York, NY 10017
Phone: (212) 486–0560
newsletter

California State Department of Education
Foreign Languages and International Studies Unit
P.O. Box 944272
Sacramento, CA 84244–2720

Center for Human Rights, New York Liaison Office
Room S–2914
United Nations
New York, NY 10017
posters, brochures, books, journals, etc.

Childreach
PLAN International USA
155 Plan Way
Warwick, RI 02886–1099
Phone: 1–800–556–7918
materials, pen pals

The Cousteau Society, Inc.
425 East 52nd Street
New York, NY 10022–6401
videos on ocean exploration

Defense for Children International
210 Forsythe Street
New York, NY 10002
Phone: (212) 353–0951
materials

Earth Flag Company
P.O. Box 108
Middleville, NJ 07855
Phone: 1–800–421–FLAG

ERIC Clearinghouse for Social Studies/Social
  Science Education
2805 East Tenth Street, Suite 120
Indiana University
Bloomington, IN 47405

The Experiment in International Living
P.O. Box 676
Kipling Road
Brattleboro, VT 05302
Phone: 802) 257–7751
citizen exchange, language training

Garrett Park Press
P.O. Box 190C
Garrett Park, MD 20896–0910
Culture Grams

Geographic Education National Implementation
  Project
1710 Sixteenth Street, NW
Washington, DC 20009

Global Learning, Inc.
1018 Stuyvesant Avenue
Union, NJ 07083
Phone: (908) 964–1114

The Grace Contrino Abrams Peace Foundation
3550 Bicayne Blvd.
Suite 400
Miami, FL 33137
Phone: (305) 576–5075
newsletter, workbooks

Greenwood Publishing Group, Inc.
88 Post Road West
P.O. Box 5007
Westport, CT 06881–5007
Phone: (203) 226–3571
quarterly publication

Institute for International Education
809 UN Plaza
New York, NY 10017
teachers exchange

International Alliance of Women
777 UN plaza, 8th Floor
New York, NY 10017
Phone: (212) 682–3649

Jalmar Press
45 Hitching Post Drive
Building 2
Rolling Hills Estates, CA 90174–4297

Joint National Committee for Languages
300 Eye Street, NE
Suite 211
Washington, DC 20002
Phone: (202) 546–7855

Junior Chamber International
P.O. Box 140577
400 University Drive
Coral Gables, FL 33114
Phone: (305) 446–7608
Model United Nations

NAFSA Publications
P.O. Box 0586
Washington, DC 20073
Phone: (202) 939–3110

The National Council for Geographic Education
Indiana University of Pennsylvania
Indiana, PA 15705
curriculum books

The National Council for Self–Esteem
6641 Leyland Park Drive
San Jose, CA 95102
activities

National Parks and Conversation Association
1701 18th Street, NW
Washington, DC 20009

National Center for Research on Cultural Diversity
University of California at Santa Cruz
399 Clark Kerr Hall
Santa Cruz, CA 95064
Phone: (408) 459–3500

National Wildlife Federation
1412 16th Street, NW
Washington, DC 20036
Phone: (202) 797–6800

The Olive Press
5727 Dunmore
West Bloomfield, MI 48322

Our Developing World
13004 Paseo Presada
Saratoga, CA 95070
teaching kits

Our Planet in Every Classroom
c/o World Federalist Association
United Nations Office
777 UN Plaza
New York, NY 10017
Phone: (212) 599–1320

Outreach Program
Jackson School of International Studies
Thomson Hall
DR–05
University of Washington
Seattle, WA 98195

Roots and Wings
P.O. Box 350
Jamestown, CO 80455

Simile II
218 Twelfth Street
Del Mar, CA 92014
RAFA RAFA—A CROSS CULTURAL SIMULATION

Social Studies Development Center
Indiana University
2805 East 10th Street
Suite 120
Bloomington, IN 47405
Phone: (812) 335–3838
Social Science Education Consortium
855 Broadway
Boulder, CO 80302
Phone: (303) 492–8154

Social Sciences Educational Consortium
3300 Mitchell Lane
Suite 240
Boulder, CO 80302–2272
Phone: (303) 492–8154
catalog

UNA/USA
Jim Muldoon, Director
458 Fifth Avenue
New York, NY 10017
Phone: (212) 697–3232
books, newsletter

UNESCO
7 Place de Fontenoy
75700 Paris, France
free magazine

U.S. Committee for UNICEF
333 East 38th Street
New York, NY 10016
Phone: (212) 686–5522
teacher kits, video, free catalog

U.S. Institute for Peace
1550 M Street, NW
Suite 700
Washington, DC 20005–1708
Phone: 1–800–537–9359
materials for general education

The World Bank
Schools Program
Publications Department
1818 H Street, NW
Washington, DC 20433
Phone: (202) 473–7529
booklets, slides, data diskettes

Appendix

These learning outcomes can be substituted for those listed under the following message: "You are a CITIZEN of the UNITED STATES OF AMERICA, a multicultural, democratic society."

◼ Rationale

As we move into the 21st century, the nation-state is the primary way human beings organize themselves on Planet Earth. Nationality and citizenship affect nearly all dimensions of one's life. People in democratic nations have special responsibilities and opportunities in fulfilling their role as citizens in locally and globally responsible ways. Children who are able to meet the global challenges confronting humankind make use of the avenues that their citizenship provides them for meeting these challenges. A globally focused curriculum provides children with a sound foundation in understanding the role of their own and other nations within a global context. Children in the United States of America, a multicultural, democratic society, focus on the cultural diversity and civic unity of the nation and its unique role in the culturally diverse and globally interdependent world.

◼ Outcomes

Learning Outcomes

In the culturally diverse and globally interrelated world of the 21st century, it is essential that students LEARN what it means to be citizens of their own nation. Children in the United States should learn about the social, cultural, and political heritage of the United States and about the people, natural environment, and culture of the contemporary United States.

Through an integrated global education, students LEARN about:

- The historical development of the United States
- The geographical features and natural environment of the United States
- The people of the United States, including the experiences and the contributions of the many ethnic groups and the emerging ethnic/cultural profile of the population
- The civic culture of the United States and the democratic principles on which the nation is founded
- Their own communities within the larger contexts of the state, region, nation, and world
- Their roles and responsibilities as citizens in interrelated local, state, national, and global contexts
- Other nations, their governments, and peoples around the globe and how these relate to and compare with the United States

---

1 Students will demonstrate knowledge about the historical development of the United States.

Cultural diversity and global connections characterize the history of the United States from its earliest beginnings. To prepare children to understand the contemporary society in which they live, the history of their nation is told not as one story beginning with the "founding" of the new nation, but as many stories of the peoples from here and around the world who figured in its creation and unfolding development. These stories, for example, portray the complexity and diversity of the pre-Columbian civilizations of the Americas and trace the coming together of the peoples of the Americas and of Afro-Eurasia to form a new nation.

Children are exposed to different perspectives on the major events and eras in the nation's history. For example, events and developments such as the Revolutionary War period, the federal period, westward expansion, early immigration, the Civil War era, the growth of industry and cities, struggles for freedom and equality, the political reform movement, contemporary immigration, and emerging postindustrial economic, political, and social systems are told not as stories of isolated events and single-dimension actors but as events unfolding in global contexts shaped by multidimensional actors representing diverse groups.

---

2 **Students will demonstrate an understanding of the geographical features and natural environment of the United States and the interactions between humans and the environment.**

The concept of the global ecosystem is essential in the exploration of the geographical features and natural environment of every nation on the planet. That the natural environment of any nation is a part of the global ecosystem and that political boundaries do not define and cannot contain environmental boundaries are two important concepts that students come to understand. Students anchor their understanding in basic knowledge about the nature and location of the physical features of the landscape and the character and distribution of natural resources. They examine and establish criteria for evaluating alternative uses of natural resources, setting their exploration in a local-global context and considering such issues as equity of access for humankind and the stability of the ecosystem.

3 **Students will demonstrate an understanding of the people of the United States, the experiences and contributions of the many ethnic groups, and the emerging ethnic/cultural profile of the population.**

The social history of the United States is rich in stories of peoples of diverse heritages and backgrounds coming together to form a new nation. Told from a global perspective, this history highlights the interrelationship of the cultural diversity of the the United States and global events and conditions. Children study the indigenous peoples of this land as well as the various immigrant groups to gain an understanding of the nation's history. They develop a growing appreciation for the ways that each historical time and setting affects "the immigrant experience" and shapes how each immigrant group responds to becoming members of this society. They begin to understand some of the ways that the changing ethnic/cultural makeup of the population may affect this society in the 21st century. They develop a growing understanding of the sources of tensions that arise among diverse ethnic/cultural groups and the conditions that reduce such tensions and bring people together.

They recognize that people from disparate backgrounds and cultural heritages have similar aspirations that bring them to a specific place. They also recognize how these commonly held aspirations help forge a nation based on common goals. They are introduced to individuals from many different heritages and economic circumstances who have been instrumental in solving social problems and shaping the character of the nation. They come to see the role that vision, planning, collaboration, and enduring commitment play in achieving better social conditions for all people.

---

4 **Students understand the civic culture of the United States and the democratic principles on which the nation is founded.**

A central purpose of education in this country has always been the preparation of citizens who can and will pursue their role as stewards of the civic culture—that public sphere where issues relating to the identification, selection, and distribution of the public resources are addressed and resolved. In a democracy, it is both the right and the responsibility of all citizens to be active participants in the civic culture, which is affected by the increasing global interdependence and cultural diversity of this society. Children in the United States who are receiving a quality education for the 21st century learn about the founding of this nation and the Constitution on which it rests; the undergirding principles of justice, liberty, and equity and the legislative, executive, and judicial government structures committed to those principles; and the struggles for justice, liberty, and equity of different groups throughout the nation's history. They learn that the central values on which this nation rests are values drawn from and shared by human beings around the globe.

5 Students demonstrate an understanding of their own communities within the larger contexts of the state, region, nation, and world.

The education of young children has traditionally begun with investigations of their immediate communities. As the 21st century comes into view, those local communities are becoming potent laboratories for learning about the world. A quality global education helps children gain an awareness of how the government, economic, religious, cultural, and education institutions in their own communities interrelate with other communities throughout the state, nation, and, the world to provide the goods and services to meet the needs of local residents. Students become familiar with the different types of communities in which people live—urban, suburban, and rural—and how communities change over time. They become familiar with the geography, resources, and government of their own state and begin to develop a basic understanding of how their community and state fit into the federal system of government of the United States. They also are exposed to the growing examples of relationships that local

communities and states are developing with communities and nations throughout the world.

6 Students demonstrate an understanding of their roles and responsibilities as citizens in interrelated local, state, national, and global contexts.

An education grounded in a global perspective is committed to providing students with well-defined conceptual maps of the many alternative routes to civic action that are open to them. Students learn that the choices they make regarding the consumption of resources within their local communities may affect not only themselves and their community, but people throughout the world. They develop the habit of thinking globally when acting locally as they trace the effects of their actions through ever more complex webs of interaction. They study examples of individual actions that have ultimately had both local and global effects, They learn to generate moral and ethical standards by which to judge action and social policy as they practice civically responsible decision making and action taking.

7 Students demonstrate knowledge of other nations, governments, and peoples around the globe and show how they relate to and compare with the United States, its government, and its people.

Children learn the differences between authoritarian and democratic governments and are introduced to the various forms of each that have been devised by different peoples throughout history and around the world. They are introduced to the theories behind diverse governmental structures and compare the theories with the actual governments that have grown out of the theories. They see the relationship between the values held by government leaders and the governmental structures and processes that develop. They begin to recognize that some governments are more responsible and effective than others in providing for the welfare of their own citizens and in participating in the international community. They study examples of citizens overthrowing repressive regimes and building responsive democratic governments. They learn of the major alliances the United States has formed with other nations to address human problems such as national security and environmental destruction and they are able to recognize the types of problems and issues that are more effectively addressed through multinational cooperation.